674.88 M513c 1987

COLUMBIA COLLEGE
674.88M513C1987   C1   VO

SO-ADF-150
3 2711 00004 5176

CREATING SMALL WOOD OBJECTS
as Functional Sculpture

New, Enlarged
Edition

ENTEREDFEB 1 5 1988

Other Books by Dona Z. Meilach

WOODWORKING
CONTEMPORARY ART WITH WOOD
CREATING MODERN FURNITURE
WOODWORKING: THE NEW WAVE

FIBERS AND FABRICS
BASKETRY TODAY WITH MATERIALS FROM
    NATURE with Dee Menagh
CONTEMPORARY BATIK AND TIE-DIE
CONTEMPORARY LEATHER
CREATING ART FROM FIBERS AND
    FABRICS
CREATIVE STITCHERY with Lee Erlin Snow
EXOTIC NEEDLEWORK WITH ETHNIC
    PATTERNS with Dee Menagh
MACRAMÉ ACCESSORIES
MACRAMÉ CREATIVE DESIGN IN KNOTTING
MACRAMÉ GNOMES AND PUPPETS
MAKING CONTEMPORARY RUGS AND
    WALL HANGINGS
A MODERN APPROACH TO BASKETRY
    WITH FIBERS AND GRASSES
PLANT HANGERS
SOFT SCULPTURE AND OTHER SOFT ART
    FORMS
WEAVING OFF-LOOM with Lee Erlin Snow

SCULPTURE
CONTEMPORARY STONE SCULPTURE
CREATING ART WITH BREAD DOUGH
CREATING WITH PLASTER
CREATIVE CARVING
DECORATIVE AND SCULPTURAL
    IRONWORK
DIRECT METAL SCULPTURE with Donald
    Seiden
SCULPTURE CASTING with Dennis Kowal

JEWELRY
ETHNIC JEWELRY

COLLAGE-PAPER
ACCENT ON CRAFTS
BOX ART: ASSEMBLAGE AND
    CONSTRUCTION
COLLAGE AND ASSEMBLAGE with Elvie Ten
    Hoor
CREATING ART FROM ANYTHING
PAPERCRAFT
PAPIER-MACHÉ ARTISTRY
PRINTMAKING

CERAMIC-TILE
TILE DECORATING WITH GEMMA

DESIGN
THE ARTIST'S EYE
HOW TO CREATE YOUR OWN DESIGNS
    with Jay and Bill Hinz

COMPUTERS
BEFORE YOU BUY A COMPUTER
BEFORE YOU BUY A USED COMPUTER
BEFORE YOU BUY WORD PROCESSING
    SOFTWARE
PERFECT GUIDE TO PERFECT WRITER
THE DYNAMICS OF PRESENTATION GRAPHICS
THE ILLUSTRATED COMPUTER DICTIONARY
    with Allen E. Meilach

EXERCISE-HEALTH
THE ART OF BELLY-DANCING with Dahlena
JAZZERCISE with Judi Sheppard Missett
HOW TO RELIEVE YOUR ACHING BACK

COOKING
HOMEMADE CREAM LIQUEURS
HOMEMADE LIQUEURS with Mel Meilach
MARINADE MAGIC

CREATING SMALL WOOD OBJECTS

as Functional Sculpture

New, Enlarged Edition

COLUMBIA COLLEGE
600 SOUTH MICHIGAN
CHICAGO, ILLINOIS 60605

by DONA Z. MEILACH

Consultant: Lawrence B. Hunter
San Diego State University, California

CROWN PUBLISHERS, INC., NEW YORK

Dedicated to:

My husband . . . Dr. Melvin M. Meilach whose
patience and put-up-with-me ability
during the gathering and writing stages of
a book are beyond the capacity of normal
human endurance.

674.88 M513c 1987

Meilach, Dona Z.

Creating small wood objects
as functional sculpture

© 1987, 1976 by Dona Z. Meilach

All rights reserved. No part of this book may be reproduced or utilized
in any form or by any means, electronic or mechanical, including
photocopying, recording, or by any information storage or retrieval
system, without permission in writing from the publisher.

Published by Crown Publishers, Inc., 225 Park Avenue South, New
York, New York 10003, and represented in Canada by the Canadian
MANDA Group

Crown is a trademark of Crown Publishers, Inc.

Manufactured in the United States of America

Library of Congress Cataloging-in-Publication Data

Meilach, Dona Z.
    Creating small wood objects as functional sculpture.

    Bibliography: p.
    Includes index.
    1. Woodwork.   2. Treenware.   I. Hunter, Lawrence B.
II. Title.
TT180.M38   1987   674′.88   87-9220
ISBN 0-517-56616-8 (pbk.)

10 9 8 7 6 5 4 3 2 1
First Revised Edition

Contents

Foreword and Acknowledgments   vi

1   The Heritage of Functional Wood Objects   1

2   Wood: Its Structure and Physical Properties   23

3   The Turned Wood Object   43

4   The Laminated Object   99

5   The Carved Object   115

6   Inlay and Marquetry   185

7   Constructing and Carving   205

8   A Gallery of Containers & Other Objects   239

Selected Bibliography   270

Wood Associations   274

Wood Publications   274

Sources for Supplies   275

Index   277

Foreword and Acknowledgments

When I first thought through the idea for *Small Wood Objects*, I visualized a book of about 150 pages—displaying perhaps 200 to 250 examples. As contacts were made with craftsmen, colleges, art schools, and designers throughout the country, the subject exploded into the present volume, with 588 photos. These examples, plus scores more that could not be squeezed in, emphasized the validity of a comprehensive investigation into this little-touched-upon area of contemporary creativity. Even as I was putting the final touches on the manuscript, museums and galleries, aware of my research, were contacting me for craftsmen whose work they could display in exhibits of "small wood objects." Wondrous things happen when an idea meets its time.

And it is certainly time to thank the many people who have contributed their individual experiences. I especially want to express my continuous gratitude to Lawrence B. Hunter, San Diego State University, California, who demonstrated several processes throughout the book and served as all-around consultant. His own examples, which I discovered during research for *Creating Modern Furniture*, were among those that inspired me to delve into small wood objects.

Milon Hutchinson of Capistrano Beach, California, deserves my award for most innovative woodworker. His workshop is a veritable museum of inventive, improvised items for original approaches to the craft. Milon and his wife, Mabel, always dropped whatever they were doing to welcome us, to show us his recent objects, and to share enthusiastically the latest solutions to his woodworking problems.

I loved the week I spent photographing objects in the San Francisco/Berkeley area, thanks to the efforts of William Jaquith Evans. With his superefficiency, he invited local craftsmen to bring their objects to "lunch" at various times during the day. We had set up a photo studio in his living room and proceeded to shoot the wildly marvelous things that were brought in by about fifteen people—many of whom stayed to see what everyone else was doing. The beauty of the experience was that many of the craftsmen knew of one another, but didn't know each other; the day ended with everyone sipping wine and swapping experiences, solutions to problems, markets, where to find sources for woods, and dates to visit at one another's studios. Thanks again, Will, for all your hospitality, including your superb Spanish omelet.

When Mel Morduant, also of Berkeley, offered to demonstrate his wood inlay methods in sleek, beautiful vases, I practically followed him home. His comments after reading the copy are ones I will treasure. I also wish to acknowledge with gratitude, the help of Rudy Hurwich, Berkeley, who drove me through the freeways and byways of Marin County to visit Espenet, J. B. Blunk, John Bauer, and others in the area. To all of them, thanks for their hospitality.

Thanks to Jocko Johnson, Capistrano Beach, California, for the demonstration with the chain saw in chapter 5. It was a revelation to see how rapidly he attacked the raw wood and changed it into a beautiful object.

A fun trip to Tijuana, Mexico, resulted in the demonstration on page 122 by Mexican craftsman José Margaro Quiroz. We had admired the carving of the Muñoz furniture factory; and when Leonard Muñoz invited us to photograph anything we liked for the book, we quickly took advantage.

We enjoyed seeing the work of the professors and students at California State University, Long Beach, California. Our thanks to the woodworking teachers, Frank E. Cummings III and John Snidecor, for your warm welcome, for showing us around, and for contributing your own marvelous examples to the book. The same thanks goes to Tom Tramel, University of California, Northridge.

My sincere appreciation to the northwestern contingent of artists who demonstrated working techniques. William E. Brewerton of Rochestor, New York, developed the series on marquetry in chapter 6. His prizewinning examples and easy approach are invaluable assets to the readers.

When Paul S. Kopel wrote about his method of making objects from clay models, interpreted into plastic foam and then into wood laminates, it was too late to return to Rochester. Thanks, Sally K. Davidson, for your excellent photographic records of both Bill Brewerton's and Paul Kopel's work.

Thanks, too, to William A. Keyser, School for American Craftsmen, Rochester Institute of Technology, New York, for your tour through the school and for the opportunity to photograph the work of your graduate students.

Stephen Hogbin welcomed me to his studio as I passed through Toronto between a workshop and a flight to Rochester. We photographed his pieces, and then both drove to the airport for trips to different destinations. Thanks, too, Steve, for sharing the drawing of your unique lathe with our readers.

I especially want to tell Barbara and Wayne Chapman of Solana Beach, California, how great I think they are. They opened their fantastic collection of art objects and permitted us to photograph anything we wanted. I was particularly eager to show historical examples that had not been seen in other books. Their selective eye and appreciation of the unusual resulted in the many objects shown that help enrich the insight into the history of the craft.

Of course, I am indebted to the individual craftsman who corresponded with me, who took and retook photos until thay were usable, and to those who shipped their work for me to photograph. Without this response and cooperation from craftsmen everywhere, the book would not be possible.

I must mention, with gratitude, the very helpful industrial sources: Edelstaal of Tenafly, New Jersey; Dremel Manufacturing Company, Racine, Wisconsin; and Merit Abrasive Products Company, Compton, California.

My thanks to my typist, Marilyn Regula, Morton Grove, Illinois, for her usual incredible analysis of my rough drafts. Thanks to Astra Photo Service, Inc., Chicago, and to Visual Productions, San Diego, for your part in processing the photos taken under the most variable conditions possible.

As always, and above all, I wish to thank my husband, Dr. Melvin Meilach, for his aid and encouragement throughout the long gathering and creative process of a book. And for his acceptance of "women's lib" long before it became a national phenomenon. And to my editor, Brandt Aymar, who has been enduring my writing ups and downs almost as long as my husband has. His luck is that he does it long distance.

Artists whose work appears in the book may be contacted for commissions or exhibitions. Direct your inquiry to the author, c/o Crown Publishers, Inc., 225 Park Avenue South, New York, New York 10003.

For this new edition, the objective was to illustrate new styles developed by artists whose work appears in the first edition and to show work by new artists. A comparison of early pieces by artists, such as Michael Graham and Frank Cummings, with their new work in the chapter 8 Gallery shows how their directions have changed. Another direction is the use of painted wood.

DONA Z. MEILACH
Carlsbad, California

All photos not otherwise credited are by Dona and Mel Meilach.

Functional wood objects have probably existed from the beginning of man's first involvement with carving wood, probably since the dawn of civilization all over the world. In Egypt, the carpenter's craft, somewhat hampered by the scarcity of good timber, was far advanced in the early dynastic period. Extant fragments indicate that in the Middle Kingdom, and more particularly during the eighteenth and nineteenth dynasties (1570-1200 B.C.), cabinetmaking attained a new excellence. Chairs, chests, and other articles of furniture were often elaborately decorated with veneer, inlay, and marquetry—all techniques still widely used today. On a smaller scale, delightful trinket boxes, cosmetic spoons and other toilet articles, gaming pieces, handles of sticks and whips were exquisitely carved in both wood and ivory and delicately painted and inlaid.

There are examples of carved wood bowls from the early Oriental cultures dating back as far as the end of the Chou period around 300 B.C., their heavy lacquer finishes evidently preserved them from the ravages of moisture and age. Because of the nature of wood, and its tendency to deterioration in moist climates, early examples are not nearly as prevalent as work in stone, ceramics, and other more stable media.

The most obvious examples of early wood objects are religious items used by many cultures and especially those that date from very early times in India, Egypt, and the Orient. One wonders whether statues of Buddha should be classed as "sculpture" or as "functional objects." But it really doesn't matter. One can safely assume that if wood was used and carvers existed, there also were myriad objects made for everyday purposes to which little value was attached by collectors until fairly recent times. Such items undoubtedly included bowls made from pieces of log for mixing grains, pipes for smoking, toys for children and for adult ceremonies, musical instruments, and household items.

Above: A Japanese *chasen*, translated as a "tea whisk," is handcarved from one piece of 5/8-inch-diameter bamboo only 4 1/2" high. Making a *chasen*, used for whipping the tea during the tea ceremony, is a highly skilled technique. It involves dipping the bamboo in hot water for a few seconds then making progressively thinner splits radially until there are about 120 divisions.
Collection, author

Right: A *wayang golek*, hand-carved puppet head used by a troupe of traveling players. Bali. 14" high, 8" diameter.
Collection, Mr. and Mrs. W. Chapman
Solana Beach, California

Opposite: Wooden box with carved decoration, on one end, representing a human face, bird figures and animals on other sides. Haida Indians, Queen Charlotte Island, Alaska, about 1850—1857.
Courtesy, Museum of the American Indian,
Heye Foundation, New York

Helmet mask from the Senufo tribe on the Ivory Coast of Africa. Called "fire spitter masks," they are used in rituals to drive away soul-eaters. The animal forms are often grotesque and highly imaginative. 40" long.
Courtesy, The Art Institute of Chicago

Bambara mask, Mali, Africa, combines carved wood with a metal forehead and cheek covering that has been indented. 13" high, 5 1/2" wide, 5" deep.
Collection, Peter Boiger, Oakland, California

Horned mask, Africa, Bapende culture, polychromed wood and raffia. 23" high, 11" wide, 9" deep.
Collection, La Jolla Museum of Contemporary Art, California Gift of Mr. and Mrs. Huston Noyes

Senufo staff (*detail*). Nineteenth century. Carved wood with metal and decorative beads. 57 1/2" high, 3 3/4" diameter.

*Collection,
La Jolla Museum of
Contemporary Art, California*

Headdress of the Simo Society, Baga tribe, Guinea. The intricately carved headpiece fits over the dancer's shoulders and is worn during fertility ceremonies.
Courtesy, The Art Institute of Chicago

Benin altar head, African culture, wood. 20 1/2" high, 9" wide, 10" diameter.
*Collection, La Jolla Museum of
Contemporary Art Collection,
Mr. Athur Bart, California*

books (see bibliography) discuss the kinds of objects made, their uses when known, and some social commentary about the times and the reasons for the object to have been made. Many of the small wood objects he deals with date from the seventeenth century. His discussion of "treen" is fascinating. *Treen* is defined in the *Oxford Dictionary* as "(i) made of 'tree'; wooden (ii) of or belonging to, obtained or made from a tree or trees—1670."

The *Encyclopaedia Britannica* states that "throughout the Middle Ages wood carving adorned every kind of church furnishing—benches, choir stalls, rood screens, altarpieces, font covers, pulpits, and lecterns—and was also employed in the decoration of small domestic articles (now known collectively as treen), including cups, spoons, molds, nutcrackers, candlesticks, boxes, pipe cases, and many others."

Mr. Pinto notes that references to treen are numerous in old English literature, particularly to chalices, cups, bowls, platters, and "services of treen." He believes that never has the term been applied to any object larger than a spinning wheel. "The term 'treen' usually described the miscellanea of small wood objects in daily domestic or farm use and in trades and professions."

Pinto's vast collection of small wood objects allowed him to observe their forms, and he subsequently wrote ". . . the above evaluation of the word 'treen' remains correct except, perhaps, to add that nearly all the objects formerly described as treen were wholly or in part the product of the turner and that most of them were one-piece objects. Where they consisted of more than one piece, the junction was made by turning means such as a lipped bowl and cover, a stem threaded or dowelled and glued into a base, as opposed to the kind of joints used in cabinetry by the carpenter. Objects intended solely for ornament such as carved figures and panels were never described as treen."

The quality of craftsmanship and the forms of the objects varied considerably by country and time. But the type of object was fairly universal among the countries of origin and includes those used in the apothecary shop and on the farm, objects for eating and drinking, items in the kitchen and laundry along with mortars, grinders and graters, costume accessories, sailors' and fishermen's devices, tools, and many more. The list is encyclopedic, particularly in Pinto's title *Treen and Other Wooden Bygones*, and should be studied by everyone interested in the heritage of the small wooden object.

Top: A Dogon lock, African culture, wood and metal, with a latch-locking device, has an animal head shaped at the bottom. 15″ high, 16″ wide, 3″ deep.

Collection, La Jolla Museum of Contemporary Art, California Gift of William Brill Foundation

Below: A contemporary hand-carved door latch by J. B. Blunk of California.

Opposite left: Chinese joss-stick holder has holes in the top to receive the sticks of burning incense. Drawers below. 10″ high, 6″ wide, 4″ deep.

Collection, Mr. and Mrs. W. Chapman Solana Beach, California

Opposite right: Jewelry chest carved from a piece of log by Dennis Morinaka with beautifully hand-modeled drawer fronts. Approximately 15″ high, 15″ wide, 12″ deep.

CONTEMPORARY TRENDS AND
COUNTERPARTS

One of the many fascinating facets in the emergence of a recognizable trend in contemporary craft circles is the application of the word *object* to small utilitarian items of any medium, whether it is ceramic, silver, glass, fiber, or wood. In Edward R. Pinto's first volume, *Treen, or Small Woodware Through the Ages*, the term "small wood object" is used throughout the book, but one feels the word "object" is a synonym for the word "item" and used as a matter of style rather than referring to specifics such as trays, bowls, candlesticks.

By the mid-1950s the use of the word *object* to signify a useful item made by a serious craftsman appeared regularly in the reviews of exhibitions and in feature articles in *Craft Horizons*, the trend-setting publication of the American Crafts Council and the Museum of Contemporary Crafts, New York. The greatest impetus that gave a "handle" to the effervescent activity was an exhibition titled "Objects: U.S.A.," sponsored by the S. C. Johnson Co., Racine, Wisconsin. A subsequent book also titled *Objects: U.S.A.* published in 1970 enabled the craftsman himself to identify his work with a "movement."

Many serious artists who turned to creating one-of-a-kind handmade crafts with unequaled fervor following World War II were no longer anonymous; they were "object makers" with status as artists. The term *handicraft* became pejorative.

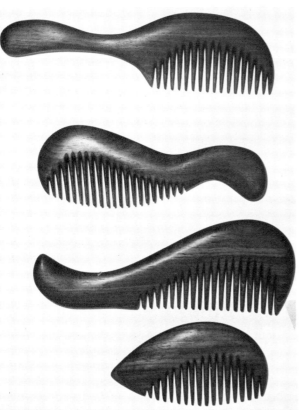

A hand-carved comb from Brazil illustrates meticulous craftsmanship and detail. 13″ high, 2 1/4″ wide.
Collection, Mr. and Mrs. W. Chapman
Solana Beach, California

Combs by Stephen R. Johnson have a contemporary curvilinear shape. Made of padouk and shedua and ranging in sizes from 3″ high, 6″ long, to 3″ high, 10″ long.

A primitive approach to the comb, still retaining a sculptural form, in the work of contemporary African craftsmen. 8″ high, 2″ and 2 1/2″ wide.
Collection, author

Opposite: Three views of a hand mirror by Frank E. Cummings III. Ebony with bone and brass. Approximately 10″ high, 5″ wide, 2 1/2″ deep. A modern interpretation of the Ashanti fertility doll.

In reality, the idea of making one-of-a-kind, beautifully formed objects by artists began with the art-craft movement that flourished in England during the latter half of the nineteenth century. Its goal was to bring art into the daily life of all social classes, and the guiding figure of the movement was William Morris (1834-1896).

Morris wished to make art part of the life of the community, to encourage the mass of society to "have nothing in your houses that you do not know to be useful, or believe to be beautiful." As he saw it, the traditional role of art had been enjoyed only by the rich and leisured class. The ideas of Morris and his associates, while not necessarily producing the socialistic trends he propounded, did have a profound influence on matters related to applied arts and architecture in Great Britain, and on the continent. From it emerged the Art Nouveau style, an international movement of "new art" which became current in Europe and the United States at the turn of the twentieth century. The use of the sinuous forms were applied to paintings and sculpture, to architecture and "applied arts," which was the name usually reserved for useful items and in direct opposition to "fine" arts. But the glass vases, wood furniture, stairwells, gates, and other applied arts were credited to individuals—they were not anonymous creations. Such names as Louis Tiffany, Victor Horta, and Henry van de Velde are well known for their contributions to the art object at this period. The Arts and Crafts Movement and Art Nouveau established the artist-craftsman in a position of status in a creative society in Europe. It took longer to reach across the ocean.

The influence of the Bauhaus school in Germany was significant to the growth of the artist-craftsman in Europe and, eventually, in the United States. Walter Gropius's organization of the school enabled the student to be trained by a painter, sculptor, and a master craftsman. He was taught to apply the same aesthetic importance to a painting, a chair, a pot, or a building. Bauhaus students were free to work in oil, yarn, ceramics, wood, or metals; and they could create objects sympathetic to the environment. An example of this total concern with design in every aspect of life was in the architecture of Mies van der Rohe and his insistence on designing the furniture for his buildings so that the total effect would be unified.

Eventually, many of these Bauhaus-trained artists emigrated to the United States where they taught at schools such as the Cranbrook Academy of

An African hand-shaped bowl utilizes some of the organic shaping of the tree in keeping with the native's reverence for the wood itself and also contributing to the design. Ebony and sapwood.

Collection, Mr. and Mrs. W. Chapman
Solana Beach, California

Elm burl salad bowl (*two views*) by Stephen Hogbin. 9″ diameter. Shaping is accomplished by placing the wood burl on a lathe. The beautiful natural mutation is effectively utilized in the design and grain.

Opposite: By Jim Traynor. An irregularly shaped, hand-carved walnut bowl shows how an unusual shape can be created from a log slab. 6″ high, 24″ wide, 20″ deep.

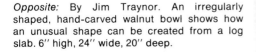

Art in Michigan, Alfred University in New York, and the Institute of Design in Chicago. Their philosophy spread. The woodworker, along with the ceramist, the glassblower, the jeweler, and other artists in various craft media voiced, more vociferously than ever, that there is no distinction between the person who produces painting and sculpture and the one who makes "objects." Their education, approach, experiences are the same: the end product is a work of art regardless of the medium used.

Many of the people whose work appears in this book helped raise the consciousness of the public to see the wooden object as a serious work of art. Some have been involved with wood since World War II and were included in the early shows and exhibits reviewed and encouraged by *Craft Horizons*. Some were furniture makers and sculptors who also created useful objects in the sculptural idiom—simply because that was how they wanted to work and the way they envisioned what a piece should look like. One of the earliest advocates of the sculptural/functional object was Wharton Esherick (1887-1970), who leaves a rich legacy of items in the Esherick Museum, Paoli, Pennsylvania. The role of the furniture maker in the history of this activity can be followed in my earlier book *Creating Modern Furniture* (Crown 1975).

Arthur Espenet Carpenter's influence has been far reaching. Following World War II he bought a lathe and began turning bowls and other treen ware. In a few years his bowls were being sold at select stores across the country and were chosen for the Museum of Modern Art's "Good Design Exhibit" in 1950. Carpenter, who uses the name "Espenet" professionally for obvious reasons, slowly taught himself the necessary skills and acquired machinery for making furniture, for which he is best known today. However, the jewelry boxes and small objects he creates "for fun" are magnificently designed with smooth, rounded surfaces and flowing lines.

Among craftsmen and a majority of knowledgeable noncraftsmen, the name of Bob Stocksdale is almost synonymous with the words "turned bowl." Bob also creates trays and platters; all his objects are outstanding for their unity of material, simplicity of form, and technique. The shape, texture, and finish of his objects are determined by the fullest exploitation of the nature of the wood and its grain patterns. He turns his bowls almost paper thin, while still retaining the essence of the form and material.

It is impossible to single out, in this book, all the craftsmen who deserve special recognition—perhaps at another time—but the objects selected for *Creating Small Wood Objects* are among the best examples of the craft as it is practiced today. The ultimate decision for inclusion was based on form, craftsmanship, variety, and use of the material. There is no distinction made between work created by established craftsmen who may also be teachers and by their students. In fact, many teachers insisted that their students submit work, often photographing the objects themselves to meet the standards necessary for presentation. The result is an almost encyclopedic foray into the contemporary wood object, its makers, and how they work.

Opposite top: Bob Stocksdale turns a bowl in the well-equipped basement workshop of his home. His bowls are known for their simplicity of design and shape and the full exploitation of the grain patterns in the wood. *At right:* a cocobolo bowl 3 1/4" high, 6 1/4" deep.

Opposite below: Arthur Carpenter (Espenet) has evolved and pioneered a variety of new forms in furniture and accessories that are visually and tactically pleasing and that use an economy of materials and stress function. The jewelry box has a pair of drawers set one within the other that slide forward and are held in place by a locking peg on the right side.

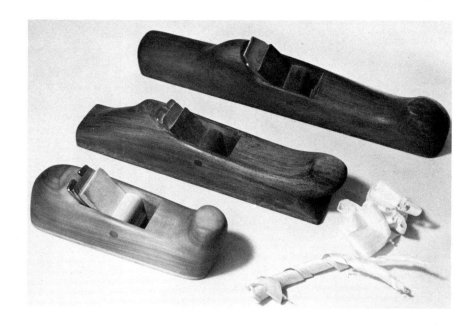

Wood: Its Structure and Physical Properties

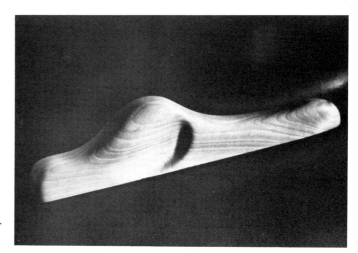

Hand-carved board push by Stephen Harris. 16″ long.

Bow, or frame, saw by Tim Ellsworth. Hickory wood.

Opposite top: The craftsman's tool storage is often handmade to custom fit manufactured and hand-shaped tools.
Photographed at Stephen Hogbin's studio Toronto, Canada

Opposite below: Three hand-carved planes by Paul Epp. Pearwood. From top to bottom, widths are 16″, 13″, 8 1/2″.

Learning the vagaries of wood is a never-ending study. A tree has basic structures and physical properties, but because of the vicissitudes of nature, each species of tree differs from another; each tree within a species will have different characteristics. Even the wood within one tree can vary and offer such variety of grain pattern, texture, and color that the chances of two objects designed, shaped, and created the same way being identical in appearance is highly unlikely.

WOOD STRUCTURE

All wood comes from trees—a perfectly obvious statement. Technology duplicates tree patterns by photographic processes on industrially made finishes, but wood itself is created only by nature. The fibrous nature of wood strongly influences how it is used. Wood is composed mostly of hollow, elongated, spindle-shaped cells that are arranged parallel to each other along the tree trunk. When a tree is cut into lumber, the characteristics of these fibrous cells and their arrangement affects such properties as strength and shrinkage, as well as the grain pattern of the wood.

In the illustration of the sectioned tree at right the basic features can be seen: 1) The outer bark which is divided into the outer, corky dead portion that varies in thickness and texture with different species and with the age of the tree, and 2) the thin, inner living bark, the "phloem" which is the pipeline through which food is passed. 3) The cambium cell layer is the growing part of the trunk which produces new bark and new wood annually. It is in the cambium that growth rings occur during the tree's early and late growing seasons. 4) Sapwood is located next to the cambium and functions primarily as the mechanical transport of water to the leaves. 5) The heartwood is the central supporting layer of the tree. It consists of inactive cells that have been slightly changed both chemically and physically from the cells of the inner sapwood rings. The heartwood varies in color and texture in various species.

HARDWOOD AND SOFTWOOD

Trees are divided into two classes: *hardwoods*, which have broad leaves, such as oak, walnut, mahogany, cherry, and ebony, and *softwoods or conifers*, which may have scalelike or needlelike leaves, such as pine, fir, hemlock, holly, and all other evergreens. The terms "soft and hard" have no direct reference to the actual softness or hardness of the wood; rather it refers to the type of cells of which the wood is composed.

Softwood is so called because it has a simple structure and is easily sawed, carved, and nailed. Each ring consists of a single type of cell, the *tracheid* or *fiber*. Seen microscopically, it is a long, slender tube, rather square in cross section with a hollow cavity. The walls of the tube are made up of two carbon compounds, the flexible *cellulose* and rigid *lignin*. The cellulose gives the wood its toughness; the lignin gives it its firmness and solidity. The center of the tube holds a small quantity of living tissue or protoplasm, but is essentially a space for transporting sap. As the sap ascends the tree trunk, it is passed from one fiber to another through minute openings known as *pits*. The types of pits found between the tracheids and storage tissues are usually quite distinctive and aid in identification of various species.

Two other features are present in most, though not all, softwoods—rays and resin. Rays run at right angles to the annual rings and radiate out from the center. In softwoods the rays are usually very narrow and scarcely visible, but in hardwoods they are very obvious. Resin is found exclusively in the softwoods. It is formed in tiny canals that exist vertically and horizontally through the wood; they have little effect on the usability of the wood.

Actual wood samples are available from several wood suppliers. Check listings in Sources for Supplies. Some have labels indicating keys for identifying woods.

Wood veneers and identifying keys can be found in source books such as *Hough's Encyclopaedia of American Woods* by E. S. Harrar. It consists of thirteen volumes showing actual veneers of transverse, radial, and tangential cuts. The volumes are available in some libraries.

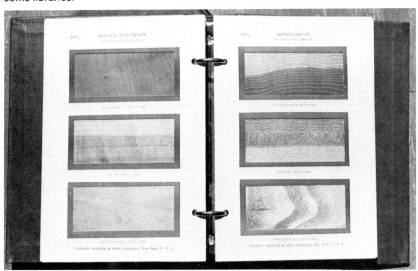

Hardwoods as a group are more highly evolved than the softwoods; their wood structure shows much greater variation in cell sizes and arrangements. It is these variations that aid in identification. The distinguishing cell type of the hardwoods is the vessel referred to as a *pore* when seen on the cross section of the wood. The individual vessels are relatively short and open at the ends; their diameters vary so that some are visible to the naked eye, others only with a microscope. Pores also vary considerably in arrangement, but two basic types appear; the pores of springwood are distinctly larger than those in summerwood.

The pores of hardwoods result in a closer grain structure than those in softwoods. This close grain characteristic inhibits splinters and chipping, making hardwoods more desirable than softwoods for carving, wearability, grain pattern, color, and texture. Rays are more obvious in hardwoods than in softwoods, often causing splits or checks as the wood dries out.

GRAIN, TEXTURE, COLOR

The variety of items created in wood attests to its versatility. The woodworker must decide upon the type of wood he wants for a specific project depending upon availability and his plans for working with it.

The grain, texture, and color of a finished piece of wood are primary considerations in selection. The terms *grain* and *texture* and *figure* are frequently used loosely or are misused. *Grain* refers to the direction of the rays or other longitudinal elements. Grain may be straight, spiral, interlocked, wavy, or irregular.

Texture refers to the relative size and variation in size of the cells ranging from fine to coarse and often to uneven. Maple, for example, has cells of small diameter, and the wood is referred to as fine textured. Oak has large diameter cells and is coarse textured. Even-textured woods have cell diameters that are very uniform, while uneven textured woods show a distinct variety in cell diameters.

Figure is another aspect of grain pattern that is determined by the way the tree grows during different seasons, the part of the tree from which the wood is taken, and the manner in which the wood is sawed.

Oak, walnut, zebrawood, and rosewood are highly grained and figured because they have a rapid summer growth period. Mahogany grows at a more uniform rate so the pattern is more regular. Ebony usually has only grain and no figure.

Unusual appearance of wood such as speckling, mottling, circling, swirling, and so on appear where the tree has grown in crotches or V-like areas, or where the trunk separates into branches. Burls, which are domelike outgrowths from the trunk caused by broken or cut branches or injuries to the tree, are highly figured because the fibers expand, compress, and encircle the area. Knots, caused by branches breaking, often are found within the tree's trunk between and within the rings. All these malformations can be used advantageously by the artist—although frequently interior injuries and growth changes in a log can also be frustrating when a project is contemplated and the unseen checks, rays, or knots interfere with the planned design.

Two kinds of grain are important to the woodworker: end grain and face grain. End grain is the result of a horizontal cut across a log. Portions of the log's rings, heartwood, and sapwood appear. Face grain runs the length of the dressed board and produces the most beautiful patterns.

Color of wood results from the presence of infiltrated compounds in the cell walls and cavities. Usually the color is limited to the heartwood and, given the thousands of different species of trees, an incredible color range may be found from the near white of holly to the jet black of ebony. The color of wood may change when it is exposed to light for long periods. In general, lighter woods darken and darker woods become lighter.

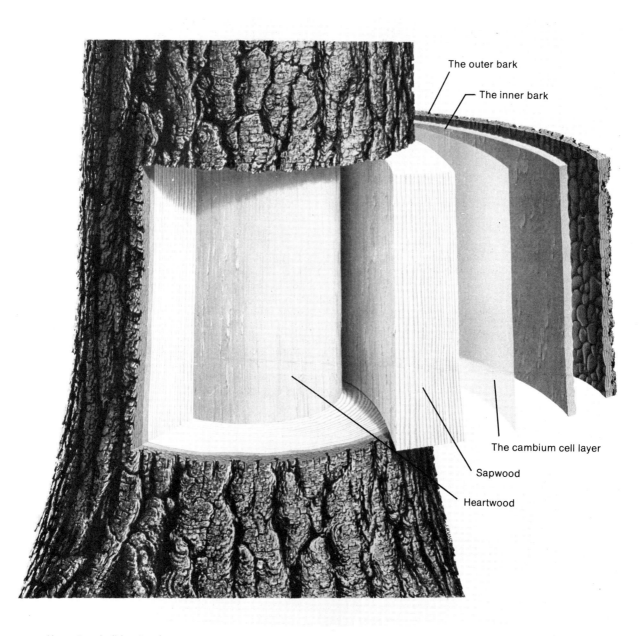

The outer bark

The inner bark

The cambium cell layer

Sapwood

Heartwood

How a tree builds a trunk.
   Courtesy, St. Regis Paper Co., N.Y.

Interestingly, very few trees have distinctive odors with the exception of cedars, rosewoods, and some firs. Usually any odors disappear after the tree has been cut down.

How cutting the log changes its appearance

Because of the way that wood is built up, it never appears the same on different cut surfaces. The way the log is cut will affect the grain pattern. A cut across the tree trunk will expose the circular annual rings and the rays show only as lines or narrow bands, or end grain (surface A). Sawing the log through the center or lengthwise, called "plain sawing," will show as highly figured lines or bands (surface B). If the same longitudinal cut is made away from the center, another pattern will result—now the rings will appear as broad stripes or patches while the rays will be narrow (surface C). A cut made on an angle to the heartwood, called "quartersawing" exhibits a linear pattern (surface D). Quartersawn wood is more expensive because there is more waste.

Veneers. Scarce and valuable woods with beautiful figuring and grain are frequently cut into veneers which are thin slices of the wood rather than board thickness. The thin veneer layers are then laminated, or applied, to the surface of cheaper timber by gluing and clamping. When you select a veneer, the stability of the veneer and the base wood are important so that neither shrinks away from the other. Veneers should be stored flat and in a dry place until they are to be used. It is also possible to create your own "veneers" of intricate laminates as shown in several examples by William Asquith Evans throughout the book. Often Mr. Evans's intricate laminates are sliced thin and placed over other woods to create the outer surfaces of his objects rather than using the laminated thickness for the entire object.

MOISTURE CONTENT AND CURING

The water content of wood is of great importance. It affects the weight, size, shape, hardness, strength, and stiffness of the piece as well as its vulnerability to attacks by fungi and insects. The water content also determines the changes in these characteristics that will occur when the wood is transported to another environment. The manner in which the wood is dried affects its usability.

A tree's moisture content may range from about 30 percent to 200 percent of the weight of the wood substance. The wood is dimensionally stable when the moisture content is above the fiber saturation point. It changes dimension as it gains or loses moisture below that point. The drying and curing of wood to minimize quick shrinking and resulting checks is extremely important. Eliminating moisture is done by careful seasoning of the cut logs. Lumber companies are able to reduce the amount of shrinkage and cracking by various production methods. Logs may be immersed in water until they are ready for the sawmill, then sawn into boards. Drying may be accomplished by placing stacked boards outdoors in the air, by kiln drying, and by radio-frequency dielectric procedures. Industrial curing methods can be further investigated in books that deal with the technology and production of lumber.

The craftsman becomes involved in seasoning wood when he gathers his own logs. The small object maker is more fortunate than the person who makes huge sculptures or gathers wood for furniture; small objects can often be made from branches that dry more rapidly than entire logs. The seasoning time generally used for air drying is one year per inch radius. Working on green wood is a waste of time.

Logs that are left to cure should be placed off the ground so they won't

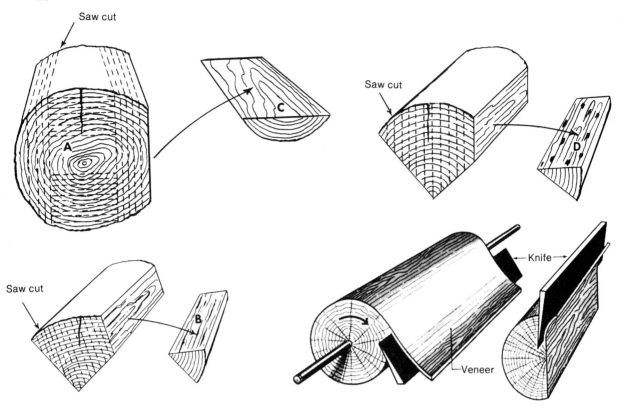

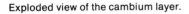

Appearances of different saw cuts.

Exploded view of the cambium layer.

The cambium layer is a single layer of living cells that extends from the tips of the tree's roots to the ends of the branches. During the tree's summer growth these cells continually divide and add only thickness but no height to the tree. The cells that form on the outside of the cambium layer become bark, those that form on the inside become wood.

Courtesy, St. Regis Paper Co.
New York

rot. In climates where winter weather and moisture are ever-present, wood is placed in curing sheds or barns to dry. Logs should usually be dried with the bark on; if the bark is removed, drying may occur too rapidly and result in severe radial checks that may begin in the sapwood and move into the heartwood. If insects exist in the bark it may be necessary to remove the bark. Insecticides may help but not always. Check manufacturers' labels for duration of insecticide life and use judiciously if objects made from the wood will be used for food. Freshly cut logs may be sealed to inhibit the rapid drying time that causes checks by brushing hot melted paraffin on the cut surfaces or covering the log ends with heavy plastic to hold in the moisture. Commercial wood sealers are also available. Only the cut ends and surfaces should be sealed, never the bark. Bark, nature's protective coating during growth, also protects the cut log from drying too rapidly.

WHERE TO GET WOOD

Logs can be secured from a variety of sources such as farms, tree surgeons, city dumps, and lumber mills. Some tree limbs have a large enough circumference for the object maker, and these can be found after heavy storms. They must be allowed to cure, of course, before using. It is a good idea to learn to identify woods to be sure they are what you want before you go to the effort of cutting, hauling, and curing them. There are several books available that give keys and charts identifying timbers by their outstanding characteristics and these are offered in the bibliography. Generally the main keys are: primary color, secondary color, pattern of growth rings, pores, grain, hardness, weight, smell, bark, shape of leaf, country of origin, and class of use.

Cut board is available from lumberyards. More exotic species can be ordered by mail from suppliers listed in the Sources for Supplies. Your lumberman should be consulted for special buys in small quantities or for individual woods he can order specifically for your use.

The creator of small objects can use old wood from houses, hotels, and other public buildings that have been hit by the wrecker's blocks. Many wrecking companies keep stacks of scrap wood left over from stair posts, fireplaces, decorative woodwork. Often, the original use of the wood will be a clue to whether it is a softwood or hardwood and what kind. Painted scrap woods will be difficult to detect, but stripping the paint from an old chest of drawers, the backboard of a bar, or other old item may reveal a bounty of good mahogany, walnut, birch, and others. Finding the source for woods, the varieties of woods, and how to work them is often as challenging as the project itself.

WORKING WITH WOOD

Woodworking tools

Wood is man's oldest and one of his most useful natural resources. From the earliest times, man has fashioned wood for shelter, furniture, tools, and weapons. The story of early tools and how their shapes were developed from iron and wood has been covered in history and technology books and in museum exhibits of primitive man—all fascinating forays into the past. Considering that man has always used tools, we tend to forget that until quite recent times he depended entirely on hand tools to fell trees and work up their timber. It is hard to conceive that the abundance and scope of woodwork in the castles, churches, and other public buildings of the Romanesque,

WOOD SELECTION CHART

SPECIES	Comparative Weights[1]	Color[2]	Hand Tool Working	Nail Ability[3]	Relative Density	General Strength[4]	Resistance to Decay[5]	Wood Finishing[6]	Cost[7]
HARDWOODS[8]									
APITONG............	Heavy	Reddish Brown	Hard	Poor	Medium	Good	High	Poor	Medium High
ASH, brown.........	Medium	Light Brown	Medium	Medium	Hard	Medium	Low	Medium	Medium
ASH, tough white.....	Heavy	Off-White	Hard	Poor	Hard	Good	Low	Medium	Medium
ASH, soft white......	Medium	Off-White	Medium	Medium	Medium	Low	Low	Medium	Medium Low
AVODIRE............	Medium	Golden Blond	Medium	Medium	Medium	Low	Low	Medium	High
BALSAWOOD.........	Light	Cream White	Easy	Good	Soft	Low	Low	Poor	Medium
BASSWOOD..........	Light	Cream White	Easy	Good	Soft	Low	Low	Medium	Medium
BEECH.............	Heavy	Light Brown	Hard	Poor	Hard	Good	Low	Easy	Medium
BIRCH.............	Heavy	Light Brown	Hard	Poor	Hard	Good	Low	Easy	High
BUTTERNUT.........	Light	Light Brown	Easy	Good	Soft	Low	Medium	Medium	Medium
CHERRY, black.......	Medium	Medium Reddish Brown	Hard	Poor	Hard	Good	Medium	Easy	High
CHESTNUT..........	Light	Light Brown	Medium	Medium	Medium	Medium	High	Poor	Medium
COTTONWOOD.......	Light	Greyish White	Medium	Good	Soft	Low	Low	Poor	Low
ELM, soft grey.......	Medium	Cream Tan	Hard	Good	Medium	Medium	Medium	Medium	Medium Low
GUM, red...........	Medium	Reddish Brown	Medium	Medium	Medium	Medium	Medium	Medium	Medium High
HICKORY, true.......	Heavy	Reddish Tan	Hard	Poor	Hard	Good	Low	Medium	Low
HOLLY.............	Medium	White to Grey	Medium	Medium	Hard	Medium	Low	Easy	Medium
KORINA............	Medium	Pale Golden	Medium	Good	Medium	Medium	Low	Medium	High
MAGNOLIA..........	Medium	Yellowish Brown	Medium	Medium	Medium	Medium	Low	Easy	Medium
MAHOGANY, Honduras	Medium	Golden Brown	Easy	Good	Medium	Medium	High	Medium	High
MAHOGANY, Philippine	Medium	Medium Red	Easy	Good	Medium	Medium	High	Medium	Medium High
MAPLE, hard........	Heavy	Reddish Cream	Hard	Poor	Hard	Good	Low	Easy	Medium High
MAPLE, soft........	Medium	Reddish Brown	Hard	Poor	Hard	Good	Low	Easy	Medium Low
OAK, red (average)....	Heavy	Flesh Brown	Hard	Medium	Hard	Good	Low	Medium	Medium
OAK, white (average)..	Heavy	Greyish Brown	Hard	Medium	Hard	Good	High	Medium	Medium High
POPLAR, yellow.......	Medium	Light to Dark Yellow	Easy	Good	Soft	Low	Low	Easy	Medium
PRIMA VERA........	Medium	Straw Tan	Medium	Medium	Medium	Medium	Medium	Medium	High
SYCAMORE..........	Medium	Flesh Brown	Hard	Good	Medium	Medium	Low	Easy	Medium Low
WALNUT, black......	Heavy	Dark Brown	Medium	Medium	Hard	Good	High	Medium	High
WILLOW, black......	Light	Medium Brown	Easy	Good	Soft	Low	Low	Medium	Medium Low
SOFTWOODS[9]									
CEDAR, Tennessee Red	Medium	Red	Medium	Poor	Medium	Medium	High	Easy	Medium
CYPRESS............	Medium	Yellow to Reddish Brown	Medium	Good	Soft	Medium	High	Poor	Medium High
FIR, Douglas........	Medium	Orange-Brown	Medium	Poor	Soft	Medium	Medium	Poor	Medium
FIR, white..........	Light	Nearly White	Medium	Poor	Soft	Low	Low	Poor	Low
PINE, yellow longleaf..	Medium	Orange to Reddish Brown	Hard	Poor	Medium	Good	Medium	Medium	Medium
PINE, northern white.. (Pinus Strobus)	Light	Cream to Reddish Brown	Easy	Good	Soft	Low	Medium	Medium	Medium High
PINE, ponderosa......	Light	Orange to Reddish Brown	Easy	Good	Soft	Low	Low	Medium	Medium
PINE, sugar.........	Light	Creamy Brown	Easy	Good	Soft	Low	Medium	Poor	Medium High
REDWOOD..........	Light	Deep Reddish Brown	Easy	Good	Soft	Medium	High	Poor	Medium
SPRUCES (average)....	Light	Nearly White	Medium	Medium	Soft	Low	Low	Medium	Medium

[1] Kiln dried weight.

[2] Heartwood. Sap is whitish.

[3] Comparative splitting tendencies.

[4] Combined bending and compressive strength.

[5] No wood will decay unless exposed to moisture. Resistance to decay estimate refers to only heartwood.

[6] Ease of finishing with clear or "natural" finishes.

[7] Prices for best grade.

[8] Leaf bearing tree.

[9] Cone and needle bearing trees.

WOOD SELECTION CHART. *Courtesy, Frank Paxton Lumber Company, Chicago*

Renaissance, and Gothic periods were all accomplished with simple tools. With our dependence upon power equipment, it is almost inconceivable that man could accomplish so much without machinery and electricity.

The Industrial Revolution encouraged the invention of woodworking machinery. The first woodworking machines are believed to have been developed in Holland as early as 1777, and a planing machine was patented in England about the same time. By the early part of the nineteenth century a wide range of versatile machines was designed to shape wood into useful products. The basic categories of woodworking machinery developed then are still essentially the same. Power, modern design, and myriad attachments have been added for further versatility. Most of the machinery can be seen in use in various demonstrations throughout the book. The woodworker can find them all pictured in catalogs and in the shop sections of department stores and machinery companies.

SAWING MACHINES: The four commonest types are:
1) The *circular or table saw.* This machine cuts wood by means of a thin circular blade with teeth around its edge. The blade which protrudes through an opening in the table can be raised or lowered to make different depth cuts. Circular saws are classified according to the blade diameter, ranging from a small 8-inch bench saw to the 14-to-16-inch saws used in lumberyards and woodworking industries.
2) The *radial arm saw* does the same kind of cutting and uses the same type of blade as the circular saw but differs in design. The motor and blade are suspended under an arm above the table and mounted so they can be moved toward or away from the operator. The arm can be turned in a complete circle. The motor and blade can be turned through a complete horizontal circle and tilted in either direction giving the saw three-dimensional movement.
3) The *band saw* blade is a continuous metal band that runs around two large wheels. The blade has teeth along one edge. The band saw is capable of only a few operations but very important ones. It can cut curves in any thickness of stock. It can also be used for resawing boards to thinner dimensions. The blade makes a narrower kerf (the cut made by the saw) than the circular saw, so less wood is wasted.
4) The *jigsaw* does the same kind of cutting as the hand coping saw, making inside and outside irregular cuts. The blade is mounted between an overhead support and a driving mechanism that produces a reciprocating movement. The blade passes through an opening in a table upon which the work is manipulated.

PLANERS or SURFACERS are single-purpose machines for smoothing woods to an even thickness. There are a variety of models that range from a single planer which smooths one surface of a board at a time to machines that can finish all four surfaces simultaneously. The planer consists of a frame, a bed that can be moved up and down, and a cylindrical cutter head that holds three or more knives that pare off the excess wood.

JOINTERS are designed to smooth the surface, edge, or end of a board. The wood is pushed along a table over a rotating cutter head that flattens the wood so that it can be made to join perfectly with another piece of wood. They do the job done by a hand plane, but more efficiently.

A SHAPER consists of a table through which protrudes a rotating spindle carrying cutting blades. The blades are shaped to produce a specific contour on the work for making moldings, edge designs on furniture, picture frames, and so on.

An assortment of woodworking machines. *Front:* The circular, or table, saw. *Back, left to right:* A drill press, a shaper (behind are pipe and bar clamps), a belt sander, jigsaw, and jointer with a shop vacuum to pick up dust particles. Safety masks hang on the wall at right.

Photographed at California State University, Long Beach

A ROUTER is essentially an inverted shaper with the cutter spindle suspended over the work. It is used for carving lines and designs in surfaces.

LATHES. Long before any other woodworking machines were invented, the lathe was used to turn out cylindrical parts. A complete discussion of the lathe and its use will be found in chapter 3.

SANDERS are used to bring wood surfaces to a fine finish. There are several types: the belt sander which has a continuous strip of sandpaper running over two rollers; a disk sander which uses a piece of sandpaper fastened to a large metal disk, and the spindle sander, a cylindrical spindle around which a piece of sandpaper is fastened.

BORING MACHINES are used to bore the holes needed for dowel joints or for pegging (page 61).

The DRILL PRESS is an upright boring machine for making holes. A drill press can be provided with a variety of accessories to serve as a spindle sander, shaper, or router, and for making small and large circular cuts, and pegs.

MULTIPURPOSE machines are designed for home workshop or school use and perform many standard woodworking operations when used with a variety of attachments. Some models combine the functions of a drill press and lathe, as well as performing sawing and sanding procedures. Others are basically jigsaws, but attachments enable one to do sanding, routing, and a variety of other small carving procedures.

PORTABLE ELECTRIC tools are designed for convenience and ease of handling. They allow the machine to be brought to the work. The assortment of power hand tools offered by different manufacturers is large and varied. The five most common portable electric tools are: the handsaw for straight cutting; the saber or jigsaw for cutting irregular shapes; the router for making joints and shaping edges, grooves, and so on; the hand drill for boring holes; and sanders of pad, belt, and rotary types.

Gluing

The use of fast-drying, transparent, permanent glues is an important factor for all types of woodworking. Many projects must have glued joints, glued members, veneers, and laminates. Some objects require gluing other materials such as plastics, metals, and papers to the wood surface. Finding the right glue to do the job is often a matter of experimentation with different types and brands. Sometimes one glue will work better on some woods than others.

Generally, the success of any glue operation is based on the following factors:
1) the adhesive selected
2) the type of wood and its proper preparation; joints must be clean and tight fitting
3) proper mixing or preparation of the glue
4) the application of the glue and the clamping operation
5) posttreatment and exposure condition of the glued member
6) the design of the joint or the laminate

The following glues are most often used by the craftsman working with small objects. Trade names vary and the same product may be packaged by different distributors. The information has been compiled by Lawrence B. Hunter.

LIQUID HIDE   Made from animal hides and bones
    Cost: Medium
    Temperature: 70° or above. Warm glue for cool temperature.
    Application: Apply thin coat to both surfaces. Let get tacky before joining.
    Assembly time: Short, about 5-10 minutes
    Clamping time: 2 hours minimum at 70°; Sears = 12 hours
    Characteristics: First choice for wherever a tough, lasting wood-to-wood bond is needed and for general wood gluing. Very strong because it is rawhide tough and does not become brittle. It is easy to use, light in color, resists heat and mold. It has good filling qualities, so gives strength even in poorly fitted joints. Not waterproof so do not use on objects to be placed outdoors.

HAND TOOLS

Hand tools such as saws, drills, screwdrivers, chisels, miter boxes, and planes are readily available from local hardware dealers in a variety of sizes.

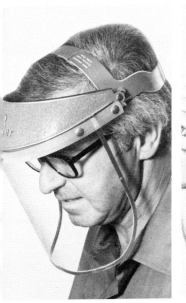

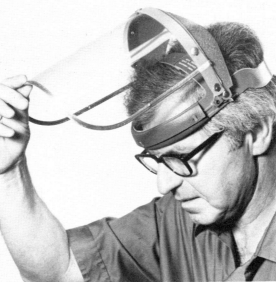

Top left: Hand tools have been used for wood carving for centuries by peoples of every culture. Different-shaped adzes are the primary tools still used by African woodcarvers to create an astonishing variety of objects.

Collection, Frank E. Cumming III
Long Beach, California

Top right: The sculptor's chisels and gouges assume an important role in the workshop of the object maker who combines carpentry with artistry.

Bottom row: Safety masks should be worn during sawing and other procedures that produce flying chips and dust. A full face mask is hinged so that in the down position it covers the entire face. It can be lifted when you are not working. Also available are goggles that fit only over the eyes and/or a pair of glasses that are held tightly to the head with an elastic band.

Courtesy, Merit Abrasive Products, Inc.
California

WHITE GLUE   White liquid resin or polyvinyl
                     Made from chemicals
   Cost: Low
   Temperature: Any temperature above 60°, the warmer the better
   Preparation: Ready to use
   Application: Spread on both surfaces and clamp
   Assembly time: Very short, 5 minutes
   Clamping time: 2 hours at about 70°
   Characteristics: A fine all-around household glue for mending. Excellent
      for model work, paper, leather, and small assemblies. Not sufficiently
      moisture resistant for anything to be exposed to weather. Not so strong
      and lasting as Liquid Hide Glue for fine furniture work. Always ready to
      use at any temperature. Nonstaining, clean, and white. Quick-setting
      qualities recommend it for work where good clamping is not possible.
      High temperatures (100°+) tend to soften this adhesive. Very excellent
      for dowel-joint gluing since this adhesive does not become brittle.

CASEIN   Made from milk curd
   Cost: Low
   Temperature: Any temperature above freezing; however, the warmer the
                     better
   Preparation: Stir together equal parts by volume of glue and water. Wait
                     10 minutes and stir again.
   Application: Apply thin coat to both surfaces. Use within 8 hours after mix-
                     ing.
   Assembly time: About 20 minutes
   Clamping time: 4-5 hours at 70°
   Characteristics: Will do most woodworking jobs and is especially desir-
      able with oily woods: teak, lemon, yew. Not moisture resistant enough for
      outdoor use. Will stain acid woods such as redwood. Must be mixed for
      each use. Works in cool locations, fills poor joints well. Casein glues will
      bond wood through a wide range of moisture contents from 2 to 20 per-
      cent. Two difficulties with casein glues are their abrasive effects on cut-
      ting tools and their wood-staining characteristics.

PLASTIC RESIN   Made from chemicals. "Weldwood," "Titebond"
   Cost: Medium
   Temperature: Must be 70° or warmer. Will set faster at 90°.
   Preparation: Mix 2 parts powder with 1/2 to 1 part water.
   Application: Apply thin coat to both surfaces. Use within 4 hours after mix-
                     ing.
   Assembly time: About 20 minutes
   Clamping time: 16 hours at 70°
   Characteristics: Use it for woodworking and general gluing where con-
      siderable moisture resistance is wanted. Do not use with oily woods,
      such as teak, or with joints that are not closely fitted and tightly
      clamped. Must be mixed for each use. Very strong, although brittle if
      joint fits poorly. Light colored, almost waterproof. Mixing of the adhesive
      is somewhat difficult. Cleanup requires soap and warm water. Shelf life
      of the powder is good unless it becomes damp.

RESORCINOL   Made from chemicals. "Bordens," U.S. Plywood
   Cost: High
   Temperature: Must be 70° or warmer, will set faster at 90°
   Preparation: Mix 3 parts powder to 4 parts liquid catalyst.
   Application: Apply thin coat to both surfaces.
   Assembly time: 30 minutes to 1 hour
   Clamping time: 16 hours

Characteristics: This is the glue for any work that may be exposed to soaking: outdoor furniture, boats, etc. Not good for work that must be done at temperatures below 70°. Because of dark color and mixing, not often used unless waterproof quality is needed. Very strong, as well as waterproof. It works better with poor joints than many glues do. Resorcinol creates a dark glue line.

EPOXY   Made from chemicals
Cost: Very high
Temperature: Any temperature
Preparation: Resin and hardener, mix in amounts stated on container.
Application: Apply to both surfaces to be glued.
Assembly time: Time varies, 1/2 to 1 hour
Clamping time: Clamping is not necessary, sets faster with heat in about 24 hours.
Characteristics: Will bond wood to metal or other dissimilar materials. Use in combination with wood, tile, metal, glass, etc. Will not shrink or swell during hardening. Waterproof, oilproof, and noninflammable. Not good for fastening wood in large products. Must be used in well-ventilated room. Avoid getting into eyes. Can be painted, sanded, filed, drilled, or machined. Can fill large holes. Excellent for poorly fitted joints. Do not use on flexible materials or where stress can peel it from the surface.

UREA-FORMALDEHYDE RESIN   Made from chemicals. Urac 185; Plyamine 21-018, Reichold Chemical Co.
Cost: Medium
Storage Life: 6 months at 70° or below. Good as long as the liquid is pourable.
Preparation: 3 parts liquid to 1 part hardener

Temperature:	60	70	80	90	100	Degrees
Assembly:	40	30	20	10	5-10	Minutes
Clamping:	12	12	6	3	1½	Hours

Characteristics: Highly water resistant, flexible, craze resistant. Excellent for furniture, plastic laminates, and veneers. Good gluing characteristics where glue-line thickness and clamping pressure may vary. Glue-line thickness to .02″ is possible. Maximum strength is reached after 5 days at 70° or above.

Spread glue on broad surfaces easily with a roller. A broad spatula or brush will also do the job efficiently.

Edge gluing is easily accomplished with the tip of a glue bottle. A bar clamp holds the laminates until dry.

CLAMPS

A variety of clamps may be employed for various gluing operations. Most wood shops are not so well equipped with the quantity and variety that Milon Hutchinson has, but knowing about clamps that may not be so readily available may help you solve stubborn and tricky gluing-clamping operations. Consult hardware catalogs for other types of clamps such as corner and mitering clamps.

Adjustable bar clamps and gluing clamps.

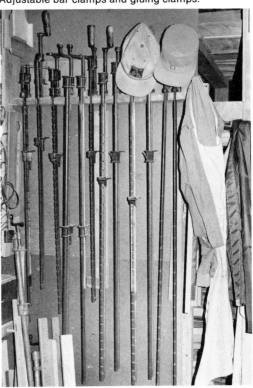

Metal-jaw bar clamps and spring clamps are on front table. C-clamps in assorted sizes hang at the back.

Industrially used lever-type clamps can be set up for convenient and quick application in the craftsman's workshop. Mr. Hutchinson has improvised and individualized boards with clamps screwed on for specific jobs.

The ultimate in the common hardwood jaw gluing clamp has been individualized by craftsman Walter C. Dreisbach who hand-carved the ends in the hand shapes.

Courtesy, artist

Wood welding

Wood welding, called "dielectric heating" is based on the fact that disturbed molecules cause friction and create heat. The disturbed balance is caused by a very high frequency cycle change which moves the molecule of glue at such a high speed that the friction generates heat and the glue bond is completed in a matter of seconds.

The synthetic resorcinol and pheno-formaldehyde resins are easily cured with dielectric heating and are relatively immune to weather conditions. Urea-formaldehyde glues are less expensive than resorcinols but have similar qualities. Joints formed with urea resins are very resistant to heat and moisture. The strength of joints made with both types of glues increases with time.

Dielectric gluing is accomplished with a wood welding unit shown on page 67.

Wood finishing

The cellular structure of wood requires the application of stains, fillers, varnishes, lacquers, paints, enamels, oils, or waxes to enhance the surface visually and totally and to protect the surface from dust and deterioration. Before applying finishes, carefully check all surfaces for dents, bumps, or stains. Sand off bumps. Raise dents by placing a damp cloth on the surface and touching it with the tip of a hot iron to expand the fibers.

Transparent and opaque wood finishes are applied by brushing, spraying, wiping, dipping, rolling, and rubbing. Finishes retard the absorption of moisture, fumes, and oils that cause the wood to shrink, swell, check, warp, and discolor.

Each woodworker seems to develop his own formula for finishing woods. The majority prefers natural oil finishes that bring out the natural grains and colors of fine woods. These vary from any proportion either side of 50-50 oil stain and raw or boiled linseed oil and turpentine to 100 percent linseed oil. Oil stains may be slightly pigmented or transparent. They are easily applied by brushing or wiping on. They preserve the wood and bring out the beauty without raising the grain and they produce a uniform tone or color.

Wood objects that will come in contact with food may be finished with vegetable cooking oils and reoiled frequently.

Varnish stains seal the wood and may produce various tonal changes without altering the grain. Aerosol foam and liquid stains offer great flexibility of application. Stains may also be made by thinning artists' oil paints with turpentine until they are fluid enough to be brushed or rubbed into the wood's surface and so penetrate the pores. Stained raw woods should be sealed with varnish, shellac, acrylic sprays, or epoxy finishes.

Coloring can be accomplished with any colorants available for wood such as enamels, paints, and acrylics. The wood must be sealed before applying the colorant. Carefully select the finish that will best serve your need; there are oil and water base, matte and gloss finishes, and the type you select will depend on the purpose of the finished item. Consider exposure to weather and humidity.

After applying the finish, a final rubbing with a fine pumice powder such as rottenstone mixed with linseed oil will reduce any fine paint bubbles or imperfections. Waxing with a good quality furniture wax is optional.

Abrasive papers

Rough sanding and fine finishing are accomplished with abrasive papers used on sanding blocks, grinders, disk sanders, stationary and portable belt sanders. Abrasive grades during the finishing stages usually progress from coarse to fine. Final finishing may be done by hand rubbing with a fine powder such as rottenstone mixed with linseed oil. When choosing abrasives, there are three points to consider:

1) Open or closed coating. On a "closed coat," the abrasive grains are closely spaced, presenting a full surface. An "open coat" has spaces between the grains so that particles removed by sanding do not fill or clog the surface of the paper. This is desirable when doing round sanding or removing an old finish.

2) Correct abrasive. The minerals used in today's coated abrasives are an improvement over the crushed seashells once used. Those most often employed are: *aluminum oxide*, a manufactured abrasive good for wood and metal. It holds up well under power sanding and is used on hardwood, aluminum, copper, steel, ivory, and plastic. *Silicon carbide*, the hardest of all abrading materials, is good for sanding undercoats and for smoothing operations between coats. *Garnet* is generally used with power tools for abrading hardwood, softwood, composition board, plastic, and horn.

3) Correct grit. Various classifications of sandpaper can be broken down in terms of coarse, medium, and fine. Manufacturers have attempted to standardize the classification and symbols used on abrasive as shown in the accompanying chart.

Abrasive papers

Mesh numbers: Abrasive grains are precision graded by passing them over a series of screens. Mesh numbers designate the grit sizes. For examples, grits that pass through a screen with 80 openings per linear inch are grit 80—designated as 80 (0). (0) is the symbol number.

MESH NO.	SYMBOL	MESH NO.	SYMBOL
600	-	100	(2/0)
500	-	80	(0)
411	(10/0)	60	(1/2)
360	-	50	(1)
320	(9/0)	40	(1-1/2)
280	(8/0)	36	(2)
240	(7/0)	30	(2-1/2)
220	(6/0)	24	(3)
180	(5/0)	20	(3-1/2)
150	(3/0)	16	(4)
120	(0)		

Courtesy, Norton Co., New York

MACHINING AND RELATED PROPERTIES OF HARDWOODS

Kind of wood	Specific gravity based on green volume & oven dry wt.	Pounds/cu. ft. at 12% moisture control	Planing perfect pieces	Shaping good to excellent pieces	Turning fair to excellent pieces	Boring good to excellent pieces	Mortising fair to excellent pieces	Sanding good to excellent pieces	Steam bending unbroken pieces	Nail splitting pieces free from complete splits	Screw splitting pieces free from complete splits
			Percent	Percent	Percent	Percent	Percent	Percent	Percent	Percent	Percent
Alder, red	.37	28	61	20	88	64	52	75	67	65	71
Ash	.54	41	75	55	79	94	58				
Aspen	.35	27	26	7	65	78	80				
Beech	.56	45	83	24	90	99	92	49	75	42	58
Birch[1]	.60	46	63	57	80	97	97	34	72	32	48
Cherry, black	.47	35	80	80	88	100	100	64	56	66	60
Chestnut	.40	30	74	28	87	91	70				
Chinkapin			75	25	77	90	90				
Cottonwood	.37	28	21	3	70	70	52	19	44	82	78
Elm, soft	.46	36	33	13	65	94	75	66	74	86	74
Gumbo-limbo			80	20	60	60	80	50			
Hackberry	.49	37	74	10	77	99	72	80	94	63	63
Hickory	.65	51	76	20	84	100	98		76	35	63
Laurel, California			40	60	86	100	100				
Madrone			90	75	88	100	95				
Magnolia			65	27	79	71	32		85	73	76
Mahogany—African	.43	31	80	68	89	100	100	37	41	68	78
Maple, bigleaf	.49	38	52	56	80	100	80				
Maple, hard	.44	33	54	72	82	99	95	38	57	27	52
Maple, soft	.57	44	41	25	76	80	34	37	59	58	61
Oak, red	.56	44	91	28	84	99	95	81	86	66	78
Oak, tanbark			80	39	81	100	100				
Oak, white[2]	.59	47	87	35	85	95	99	83	91	69	74
Pecan	.60	47	88	40	89	100	98		78	47	69
Sweetgum			51	28	86	92	58	23	67	69	69
Sycamore	.46	35	22	12	85	98	96	21	29	79	74
Tupelo			55	52	79	62	33	34	46	64	63
Walnut, black	.34	26	62	34	91	100	98		78	50	59
Yellow-poplar			70	13	87	87	63	19	58	77	67

[1] Includes yellow, sweet, and all other commercial birches except white or paper birch.
[2] Includes chestnut oak and other commercial white oaks.

Comparative physical properties of some popular woods. Data for this chart is from the U.S. Forest Products Laboratory and compiled by the Fine Hardwoods-American Walnut Association, Chicago, Ill. A more complete chart is available from the Fine Hardwoods-American Walnut Association booklet "Fine Hardwoods Selectorama."

The Turned Wood Object

Opposite: By Jim Traynor. Lathe-turned and hand-finished wine decanter of East Indian rosewood. 8 1/2'' high, 3 1/2'' diameter. The goblets are exquisitely shaped, with British gray harewood cups and East Indian rosewood stems. (*See color photo for the complete table setting.*)

Right: A bud vase by Jim Traynor. Rosewood with shedua laminate and inlay, lathe turned. 12'' high, 3'' diameter.

Below: A simple, elegant, turned teak vase by Mel Mordaunt utilizes the grain pattern to emphasize the shaping. 4 3/4'' high, 4'' diameter.

The turned object refers to one that has been shaped on a lathe, perhaps one of the most versatile tools in the woodworker's shop. With the lathe, a block of wood can be quickly carried from rough form to finished work, including roughing, scraping, cutting, shaping, sanding, and oiling. The types of objects usually made on a lathe are spindles, bowls, cups, weed pots, bottles, beads, plates, and any items that fall within this shaping. The lathe also can be used to make asymmetrical turnings, ovals, and a variety of odd forms within the limitations of the tool's capabilities and the operator's capacity to experiment and improvise.

The lathe is a machine with two "centers" on a common horizontal axis between which material is held and rotated while being shaped with a variety of cutting tools. In addition to working material mounted between the two spindles, work can be mounted on faceplates which attach to the "live" or rotating center, so that flat projects such as bowls, plates, and hollow containers can be formed. Manufactured and improvised jigs may be attached in such a way that the work mounted on the lathe can be drilled and cut into in various ways, and its surface can have pegs, other wood inlays, and decorative embellishments.

The principle of the lathe has not appreciably changed since it was, reportedly, invented in ancient Egypt except that electric motors have replaced the hand or foot power used to turn the spindle. It still remains a means of turning work at controlled speeds, so that sharp tools pressed against it will cut it to a shape. The quality of the output depends on the forms the operator envisions and his skill in manipulating the chisels to release that vision from the rough block.

Wood lathes are designated according to the maximum diameter of work that can be swung over the bed; a lathe capable of swinging an 11-inch diameter disk of wood is called an 11-inch lathe. The terms *wood lathe* or *speed lathe* are usually used to avoid confusing them with screw-cutting, metal-turning lathes. The essential parts of the lathe are the *headstock*, the *tailstock*, and the *tool rest*. The two main attachments are the *spur center* that fits the headstock spindle and is known as the *live center* and the *cup center* that fits the tailstock spindle and is known as the *dead center*. The live center in the headstock serves as the driving unit that rotates the work while the dead center supports the opposite end. Attachments such as drill bits and boring units can be placed on the tailstock for making holes in ends and through the work.

Before operating a lathe, one should consult the manufacturer's directions and locate all the parts, learn how they work, and what they can do. For example, an indexing mechanism accurately spaced around the rim of the drive pulley can be used for spacing cuts in fluted work, for pegged inserts, and for dividing faceplate work.

One should understand the different rotating speeds. A good manual or handbook on the use of the lathe will inspire its application for asymmetric turnings and unconventional uses of the tools. Some are shown in relation to specific projects in this book, but it is wise to research many sources to spark additional ideas for your own work.

Tools: The standard set of tools used in wood turning includes five different shapes. Most important of these is the *gouge*, a roundnose, hollow chisel that can be used for any cutting action and especially for roughing cuts, cove cutting, turning work from square to round, and other operations. Next in importance is the *skew*, a double-ground flat chisel with the end ground to an angle instead of being square across. This tool is designed to cut, shear, and scrape and is used for smoothing cylinders, cutting shoulders, beads, V grooves, and so on. The *spear* or *diamond point* chisel and the *roundnose* are *scraping* tools used where their shape fits the contour of the work. The *parting tool* is a double-ground chisel used with a scraping action for cutting off and for making straight incisions or sizing cuts to any required diameter. All tools must be kept in optimum sharp condition.

The lathe is set on a table that can be either
stationary or placed on wheels for mobility.
Larry Hunter has utilized space beneath the
table by building a holder for the tools where
they are easily and safely accessible.

The parts of the lathe

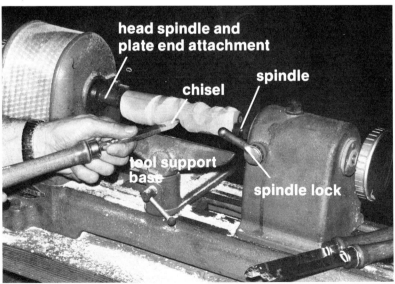

The *tool rest* consists of two main parts—the base and the tool rest, or support, itself. Different types of rests are interchangeable in the same base. One tool rest clamps onto the lathe bed and is used for turnings mounted between the spindles or on the headstock for chuck spindle turning. A floor stand for the tool rest is available for faceplate turnings. The tool rest should be about 1/8 inch away from and 1/8 inch above the work centerline.

The tool rest is designed to facilitate correct use of the hands and position of the tool. The back of the working hand, or a portion of it, rests on the finger ledge. The other fingers are placed comfortably around the tool. The other hand holds the handle of the tool and provides the movement that determines the cut. Generally the hand on the blade provides the action and the feed pressure, while the other hand acts as a control. Consider the area of the tool rest on which the chisel sits as a pivot point that is held by the thumb and fingers while the hand on the handle as actual control of the cutting edge.

The feed of the tool determines the amount of wood removed. It should be slow and steady, never forced or jabbed into the work.

There are three basic cutting actions—*scraping, cutting,* and *shearing.* Of the three, the *scraping* action is probably the easiest and most often used. The tool is held on a horizontal plane and moved directly forward into the work until the cut is the necessary depth. The full depth does not have to be reached at once. The chisel can be moved forward slightly, then moved from side to side, pivoting it on the point, achieving a shape at the same time the cut is being made.

For the *cutting* action, the tool edge is brought up by lowering the handle end of the chisel. The cutting action takes practice to master: if it is not done properly and the tool is jabbed into the wood too suddenly and deeply, it can be wrenched from your hands or you may lift a large splinter out of the work. But once the cutting action is mastered it can leave a surface smooth enough to be finished with little additional work.

A *shearing* action is usually accomplished with the skew and the gouge. It is like a cutting action with the tool moved parallel to the work as it shears away a layer of wood from the surface of the stock.

While each tool is intended for certain operations, their use can overlap and your choice of which tool to use for which job will depend on your facility, the cut to be made, and your eventual preference after you have practiced with them and their handling becomes second nature.

Safety. The lathe is a safe tool. The ultimate rule is never, never to work with dangling clothing such as neckties, necklaces, frayed or dangling sleeves, or with long, loose hair. Keep lathe chisels behind you or off to one side when you work so you won't have to reach over the turning work for a chisel when you need it. Never use your fingers to check the work for smoothness or roundness while the lathe is turning. Keep your chisels sharp for easy cutting, mount the work securely and run at the proper speed for the size of the work as indicated. Be sure the power switch is safely and easily accessible and attach a foot switch for ultimate convenience and safety.

The proper working position for lathe cutting
is shown. The tool is held with one hand on
the blade, the fingers resting on the tool rest.
The other hand supports the handle which
can be placed against the hip for stability.
The handle is slightly lower than the cutting
blade.

Basic and modified lathe cutting tools are:
A. Large, modified roundnose
B. Roundnose
C. Skew
D. Large gouge
E. Small gouge
F. Parting tool

G. Modified skewer
H. Roundnose from a file (ground on a
   grinder)
I.&J. Small roundnose forged from tool steel
K,L,M. Small lathe tools shaped on a
        grinder to various shapes for in-
        tricate work

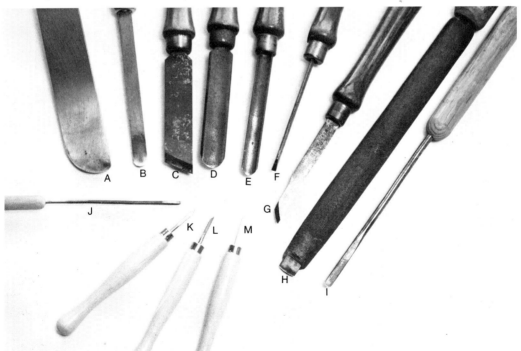

Opposite: A few of the myriad types of items
that can be turned on a lathe include spindles, furniture legs, tool handles, drawer and
door pulls, mallets, dishes, and bowls.
                    Courtesy, American Edelstaal, Inc.
                         Tenafly, New Jersey

GRINDING AND SHARPENING

Lathe tools should be kept sharp for optimum cutting action. A grinding attachment is available for the headstock of the lathe; the tool rest can support and provide an adjustable base for mounting platforms made especially to hold particular tools. Or use a general purpose grinding wheel of a 60 grit aluminum oxide about 5- to 6-inch diameter. Always wear safety goggles when sharpening tools.

With the grinding wheel revolving toward the operator, the tool is held low and gradually raised to a position in which the bevel will lie flat on the stone. This angle is maintained throughout the grinding operation. The roundnose, because it is convex on the outside, must be rolled and worked from one side of the stone to the other.

Continue to work the edge until the proper cutting angle is achieved. A burr must remain on the roundnose because it is essentially a scraping tool.

A burr can be reset by passing the tool on the concave side of a honing stone. When any tool used for scraping is sharpened, the burr should be left on. Cutting tools would have the burr removed through honing.

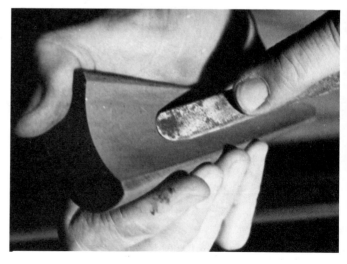

LATHE SPEED GUIDE FOR WOOD TURNING
Follow these recommended lathe speeds as nearly as possible. Change lathe speed only with the spindle in motion.

On pieces over 10″ diameter, keep the speed below the point where the lathe begins to vibrate.

LATHE: WOOD TURNING
Speed range of lathe: 230 RPM to 2100 RPM

DIAMETER OF WORK	OFF ROUGHING	CUTTING GENERAL	FINISHING
Under 2″	900 RPM	2100 RPM	2100 RPM
2″ to 4″	700	2100	2100
4″ to 6″	700	1200	2100
6″ to 8″	500	800	1250
8″ to 10″	350	700	900
over 10″	230	350	600

Detail showing the proper edges of standard lathe-turning tools. Angles should be retained accurately when sharpening.

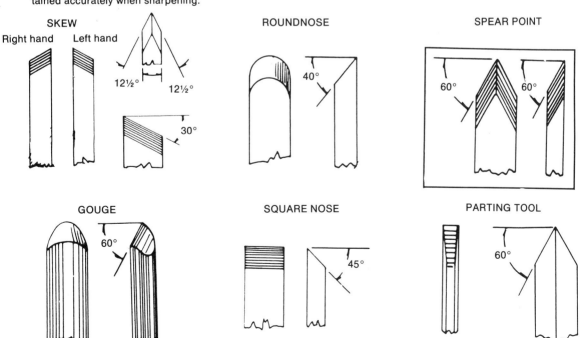

SKEW
Right hand   Left hand
12½°   12½°
30°

ROUNDNOSE
40°

SPEAR POINT
60°   60°

GOUGE
60°

SQUARE NOSE
45°

PARTING TOOL
60°

There are many manufacturers of lathes. One usually thinks of a large unit that requires an ample workroom setup. A miniature unit that is used by several of the craftsmen whose work appears in this book is one which can be set up on a small worktable when space is limited. The Unimat, an amazingly versatile machine, has all the features of a large precision unit on a small scale. A variety of attachments can alter its performance as a lathe to a polisher grinder, drill press, vertical mill, or surface grinder. Available accessories include a planer, jointer, and other woodshop needs.

UNIMAT set up as lathe
Courtesy of American Edelstaal, Inc.
Tenafly, New Jersey

For spindle turning, a paper layout can be used for making several shapes the same.

51

The wood is placed between the tailstock and headstock and turning begins using a scraping tool to shape and smooth.

Sanding can be accomplished while the object is on the lathe.

A grinding wheel accessory attached to the headstock can be used to sharpen tools.
UNIMAT setups in use
Courtesy of American Edelstaal, Inc.
Tenafly, New Jersey

TURNING A BOWL ON THE FACEPLATE

Turnings such as spindles, beads (see page 86), table legs, and posts are mounted between the two centers of the lathe. The shape may be formed in any limited area or along the entire length of the stock. Not all lathework is mounted between centers. Such items as bowls, plates, lamp bases, and so on must be mounted on a faceplate, attached only to the live center in the headstock.

Bowls are among the challenging and popular forms that craftsmen tackle. Large bowls are turned on the outboard end of the headstock. The method is demonstrated by Lawrence B. Hunter. Several examples of bowls created by many craftsmen follow the demonstration. After the bowl is turned, further designing, shaping, and surface decoration may be accomplished by direct carving with hand or power tools.

All cutting in faceplate work is done by scraping; any attempt to use a cutting technique on the edge grain of large work will result in a gouging cut that may pull the chisel out of your hands. The tool rest is placed on a floor stand.

The stock used may be from a log that has been roughly cut to shape on a band saw, from a block of solid wood, or from a block of laminated wood pieces.

Once the faceplate is mounted you should establish dimension lines for the depth of the cut and the thickness of the walls of the bowl. Dividers and compasses are helpful in measuring the work as it progresses and templates may be used as in spindle turning.

For reaching into deep, hollow projects, the straight tool rest is not always adequate support. Larry Hunter has fashioned a curved tool rest (page 55). In the series on page 61, photo shows how Milon Hutchinson has created a jig with a small blade for cutting deep, hollow interiors. It is possible that every woodworker who turns bowls has solved the problem in his own ingenious ways. These or any solutions may be adapted to your own working methods.

The following series is: a) mounting the faceplate to the end that will be the top of the bowl and finishing the base completely. b) Changing the faceplate to the finished base and then working the interior. The bottom is worked first because once the interior is hollowed out from the top of the bowl, there is no surface to which the faceplate may be attached for finishing the base.

The 6-inch faceplate is centered and screwed to a block of English walnut 7″ high and approximately 12″ in diameter. It is placed on the lathe and hand turned so that a pencil line circumference can be determined for the exterior diameter.

Above: The block is placed on the band saw and the excess diameter is cut away. The diameter is now 10''.

Right top: The block attached to the faceplate is placed on the outboard end of the headstock and scraping of the base begins. (*See photo page 54 for overall working position.*)

Right center: The base of the bowl begins to evolve. The roundnose is used exclusively with a scraping action.

Right below: The bottom is finished as much as possible. Sanding is accomplished with sanding disks mounted on a 1/4-inch drill. A flexible sanding disk is invaluable for achieving the subtle curves desired. Mr. Hunter attached a circle of 1/8-inch Masonite to a 1/4-inch bolt which is placed in the chuck. A slab of foam rubber is glued to the Masonite. Then a circle of inner tubing is glued to the foam. Use a strong glue for Masonite, foam, and inner tubing. A sanding disk is lightly glued to the inner tube so it can be changed easily. The sanding drum can be moved in any direction. One can make these in a range of diameters from 2'' to 6''. Hard disks already mounted to a bolt can be purchased and then fitted with the foam and tubing.

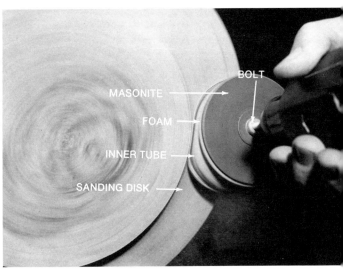

BOLT
MASONITE
FOAM
INNER TUBE
SANDING DISK

Above: a) The bottom is completed. The 6-inch faceplate is placed against the bottom and marked for central placement and holes. b) The holes are made with a drill. c) The faceplate is screwed on securely. When the bowl is completed the holes will be filled in with particles of sanded wood mixed with Duco cement (see page 78).

Mr. Hunter shows the working position and tool setup for outboard faceplate turning. He is beginning to scrape down the exterior shape. As the work proceeds, it's a good idea to take it off the lathe occasionally and set it upright to determine how the shape is evolving.

He begins to cut into the center to release the rim. When the tool dulls it must be sharpened on a grinder.

The rim is established so that hollowing out may be done. Cutting into this much wood is a slow procedure that should not be rushed.

He proceeds to hollow out the center. Instead of the straight tool rest, which does not give adequate tool support for deep interiors, Mr. Hunter uses a rounded rest which he made from a piece of scrap steel found in a junkyard to which he welded a piece of curved steel rod. Final sanding and oiling may also be done on the lathe (see pages 51, 77, and 88).

Demonstration, Lawrence B. Hunter
Photos, author

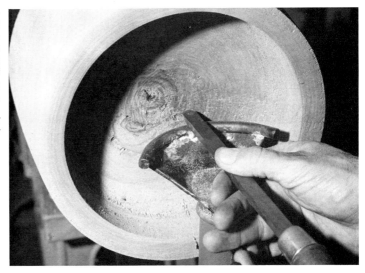

Above: By Dan L. Valenza. Turned bowl of walnut,
El Salvador Group. 8″ high, 11 1/2″ diameter.
Collection, Smithsonian Institution
Photo, artist

Left: By Lawrence B. Hunter. Shedua. Lathe-turned
bowl with hand-tooled gouge texture on outside.
3″ high, 14″ diameter.

Right: By Bob Stocksdale. Zebrawood with concen-
tric circles. 4″ high, 7 1/4″ wide, 6 1/2″
deep.

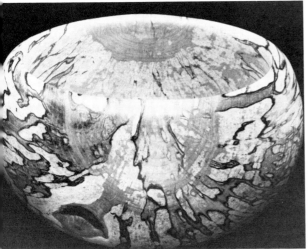

Above: Laminated walnut bowl by Charles M. Kaplan, 5″ high, 15″ diameter.

Photo, artist

Below: By Mark Lindquist. Turned spalted yellow birch bowl. 5 1/4″ high, 10″ diameter.

Photo: Bob LaPree

Above: By Lawrence B. Hunter. Bowl of worm-eaten California pepper. 4 1/2″ high, 7″ diameter.

Below: By Melvin and Mark Lindquist. Turned wild cherry burl bowl. 6″ high, 8″ diameter.

Photo, Bob LaPree

Above: Box by Milon Hutchinson. A round interior with a cover within a square base. Vermilion and padouk. 3 1/2" high, 7 1/4" square.

Below: By Lawrence B. Hunter. Teak. 7" high. Graduated bowls up to 14" diameter. The lathe-turned pedestals are carefully designed to form tiers.

Left above: By Irving Fischman. Bowl of laminated walnut, zebrawood, and teak. 9" high, 9 1/2" diameter. The shape is based on native American basketry concepts. *Courtesy, artist*

Left center: By Keith E. Stephens. Turned teakwood bowl with hand-carved exterior. 4" high, 12" diameter.

Left below: Miniature corked jars and vase by Jay O'Rourke. Various woods: cocobolo, rosewood, Burmese padouk, osage orange, shedua. Vase is 2" high, 3/4-inch diameter. Jars range from 1 1/4" high, 1-inch diameter to 2" high, 1 5/8" diameter.

Three bowls of entirely different shapes made on a lathe. By Lawrence B. Hunter. English walnut. Sizes are 4″ high; 7″, 8″, and 10″ diameter.

Below: Mr. Hunter shows the method used for achieving the exterior texture with a narrow-blade gouge.

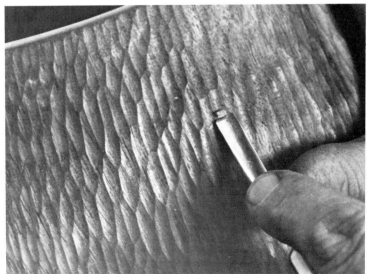

TURNING A JAR SHAPE

Deep narrow boring is required for jars, boxes, and similar containers, and these may be done on the outboard of the faceplate as shown in the previous demonstration or on the inner turning spindle as illustrated here.

An item is placed on the turning spindle by any chucking method that will hold the cylinder firmly so it can be bored on the inside. The wood can be screwed directly to the faceplate. Another method is to glue a piece of paper between a piece of scrap wood and the turning wood. The latter procedure results in a perfectly finished bottom without the need for screw holes to be camouflaged and filled in later.

The following shows the methods for making deep borings with the object mounted on the inner turning spindle. You can proceed by cutting away the interior with lathe tools or by boring a hole in the center with a drill press and then using the lathe tool to work outward. Or you can devise your own tools such as that demonstrated at far right by Milon Hutchinson.

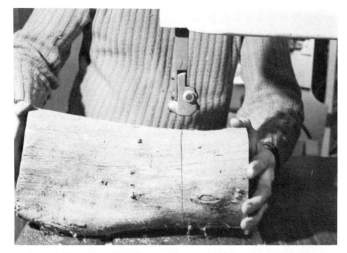

The wood piece is cut from the log on the band saw.

A piece of wood may be mounted so there are no faceplate screwholes in the finished base. The faceplate is mounted and screwed to a piece of scrap wood. A circle of paper is glued between the scrap wood and the wood to be turned, then clamped and allowed to dry thoroughly. After turning, the woods are separated at the paper line (see page 76, punch cup base demonstration).

Boring into the central opening is accomplished with the wood turning on
the headstock spindle. The tool rest is
clamped in the lathe base and moved
to the necessary height and angle.
The exterior of the shape is also cut
while mounted in this fashion. All cutting is done by scraping with the
roundnose, skew, or spear tools.

Because boring is a slow process that
requires hand-holding the tool for
long periods, Milon Hutchinson created a boring bar with a tool-steel cutting blade (see below) that simulates
the cutting action of the lathe tool. It
enables you to achieve a greater
depth and a cleaner cut interior than a
hand-held tool. The boring bar is
made from a piece of curved pipe that
is directed into the hollow by hand.
The cutting action occurs along the interior side of the object as the blade is
moved in and out. An adjustable stop
ring (just next to hand in photo) adjusts the depth of the cut.

The crank, lower left, turns in a
clockwise movement and adjusts the
horizontal position of the boring bar.
First a hole is drilled into the center of
the object with a drill, then the hole
can be quickly and easily enlarged
with the boring tool.

The apparatus is made so that it is
locked into the lathe bed with a wing
nut, bottom right. Another lock fits
through from the top for securing it to
the lathe.

Below: In the circle you can see the
blade which is a piece of cutting steel
from a metal lathe that will cut metal
as well as wood.

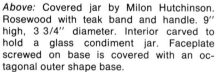

Above: Covered jar by Milon Hutchinson. Rosewood with teak band and handle. 9″ high, 3 3/4″ diameter. Interior carved to hold a glass condiment jar. Faceplate screwed on base is covered with an octagonal outer shape base.

Top right: By Lawrence B. Hunter. A covered container with a rosewood bottom and lignum vitae top. Leather lining. 5″ high, 4 1/2″ diameter.

Below right: By Lawrence B. Hunter. Turned bowl of avocado wood with chip-carved exterior. 4″ high, 5″ diameter.

Above: By Keith E. Stephens. Myrtlewood bowl and box. Each 5″ high, 5″ diameter.

Below left: By Charles M. Kaplan. Laminated cherry and walnut bowl. Lathe-turned interior, hand-carved exterior. 7″ high, 9″ diameter.

Below right: By Jocko Johnson. Ironwood cup. Interior machine turned with hand-carved base. 6″ high, 4″ diameter.

DECORATIVE PEGGINGS

Many of the objects shown throughout the book have decorative surface treatments made by pegging, inlay, painting, nailing, carving, and so forth. In this demonstration, Milon Hutchinson shows the application of a variety of inlaid plugs, some in single and some in double rows; some double cut one within another. Mr. Hutchinson applies this plugging to jars and bowls. In several, the plugging appears only on the outside, in others, they go all the way through. In other motifs, only some of the plugs appear on the interior and exterior. The range of possible combinations is unlimited.

Such plugging must be measured accurately and spaced, or indexed, around the object. The main procedures that must be accomplished are a) indexing, b) boring the holes, and c) making and placing the pegs.

Indexing can be accomplished in several ways, and Mr. Hutchinson demonstrates indexing with a circular indexing device that he has devised and with the lathe. He demonstrates boring holes on the boring machine and on the lathe. Indexing and boring can also be accomplished on a drill press but not as accurately or easily as on the other two tools. Pegs can be made from ready-made dowels or created with the plug cutter as shown in photos on page 66. Then they are hand-set. Plugs are placed in the partially turned object. After the plugs are set, final turning is done to smooth the plugs on the outside, and on the inside where necessary.

Pegged inlay jars hold glass liners for jelly or other foods. By Milon Hutchinson. *Left jar:* Monkeypod with teak peg inlays and Brazilian rosewood lids. *Right jar:* Monkeypod with a purpleheart lid. The outer circular inlay is rosewood with a white maple inner plug. 6″ high, 2 3/4″ diameter.

An indexing ring with holes bored around the circumference is clamped to the adjustable table of the boring unit. The object is secured to the indexer by a tight-fitting inner chuck. The boring machine is set at a 1/2-inch depth cut and the drill is 5/8 inch.

An index locking lever is used, *at right*, to secure the unit while the hole is being bored. The adjustable table permits the unit to be raised and lowered to make holes at different levels in the object without replacing and realigning the indexer.

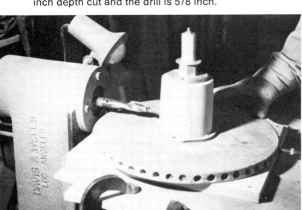

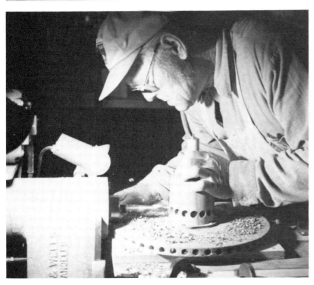

Mr. Hutchinson checks the progress of the drill along the marked lines. It is easier and more efficient to drill with an object flat on a table than holding it up in a drill press.

When the boring of the first row of holes is completed, mark the object in relation to the table so that you can replace it in the same position if you wish to do a second row of holes, or of smaller holes within the first pegs.

The bored holes are ready to receive the pegs. Pegs are quickly made using a 5/8-inch plug cutter along a 3/4-inch strip of wood.

When a series of plugs are cut, the strip is run through the blade on the table saw. Store extra pegs of each type of wood in jars labeled with name of wood and diameter of peg.

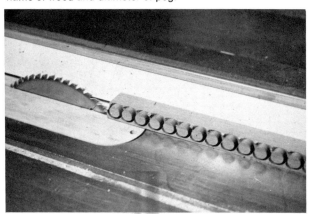

An industrial glue, San-o-Lac, is distributed around the edge of the hole with a dowel of a smaller diameter than the hole.

The pegs are driven into the hole with a hammer. Plugs are usually contrasting colors and grain for distinctive variations.

If plugs are too tight sometimes an air compression occurs and the plug blows back out. The peg can be seated using a C-clamp for a few seconds until the compressed air dissipates.

After all plugs are seated and thoroughly dried, the jar is placed on the lathe for final turning and smoothing around the pegged area and anywhere else additional shaping is desired.

Gluing can also be done with an electronic glue welder which heats and dries the glue instantly. (Hand gluing requires that you wait for the glue to dry before finishing on the lathe.) The electronic wood welder works with heat induction and requires a special glue. On this jar, one series of pegs has been finished flush with the jar, and a second series of pegs has been inlaid partially within the first series.

Demonstration: Milon Hutchinson
Photos, author

All items on these pages are by Milon Hutchinson and illustrate various applications of decorative pegging.

Above: Bowl of African laurel with a single row of rosewood pegs. 1 5/8'' high, 7 1/2'' diameter.

Left: Covered jar of monkeypod with teak and Brazilian rosewood pegs and rosewood lid. A single row of pegs is at top of body, a double row of superimposed pegs at bottom. First a row of 1/2-inch pegs were worked in, then overdrilled with a row of 5/8-inch pegs. A matching double peg is in top center of lid.

Opposite top: A rosewood bowl with teak inlay. 1 5/8'' high, 9'' diameter. The first row of pegs was placed through the bowl rim to show on inside and out. The second row was inlaid only in the outer surface of the bowl.

Opposite below: Teak bowl with rosewood inlay. 5 1/2'' high, 7 1/2'' diameter. Elongated pegs were cut on a drill press. Indexing and boring also accomplished on the drill press.

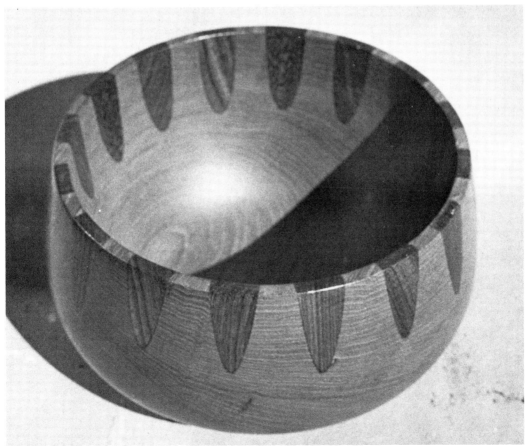

In this series Milon Hutchinson shows how a bowl is mounted, indexed, and bored using the lathe.

The bowl blank is held to a piece of scrap wood using glued paper sandwiched between. The scrap wood is mounted to the faceplate.

Indexing is accomplished using the indexing dial on the lathe.

The bowl block is mounted on the lathe and, as the indexing unit is spaced (*left*), a line is drawn on the bowl using the tool rest as the ruler. Here one set of holes has been bored and lines are indexed for the second set which will be placed between and slightly below those in the first row.

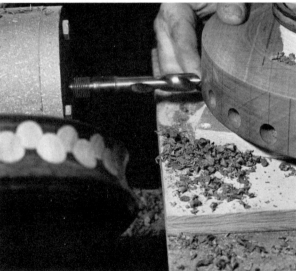

With a boring unit the holes are drilled around the circumference of the bowl with the bowl placed in a horizontal position. The result will be the double inlay peg shown in the bowl edge held at left in the photos and in the finished bowl (*top of page 69*).

When a boring machine is not available, holes can be made using an improvised setup on the lathe. First, holes are bored in a small block of hardwood such as maple, using a drill press with the desired diameter bit. The piece then serves as a jig, and it is clamped to the tool rest so the hole lines up with the position of the bowl set up on the inner center of the lathe.

The bowl is positioned and tightened, and the hand drill is worked through the hole in the jig into the bowl. Put a stop washer on the drill bit so it stops at the depth desired.

Mr. Hutchinson has also developed a method for drilling square holes. He made a special fixture for use on the boring machine. Using a square mortising tool from the drill press, he outfitted the end fixtures so they could be placed on the boring machine. A drill bit is placed within the mortising tool. When the bit is worked into the wood, the mortising square punches through resulting in a square hole that is then inlaid with square dowels. The bowl, *right*, still on the lathe shows the combination of round and square pegs inlaid.

Demonstration: Milon Hutchinson
Photos, author

By Mel Mordaunt. Maple vases with various inlays. *Left:* a pau ferro line and maple center. 3'' high. *Center*, Padouk inlays. 5'' high. *Right*, Brazilian rosewood inlays. 3'' high. All 3 1/4'' diameter.

Courtesy, artist

Mel Mordaunt has developed methods for insetting various geometric shapes of different woods in his beautifully designed weed pots. He says, "I like my work to be simple, clean, and crisp rather than ornate or complicated. Within this structure I wanted some sort of surface decoration. This solution was inspired by some of the Swedish glass designs with a symmetrical motif repeated around the circumference."

To accomplish insets, Mr. Mordaunt uses a router guided by an improvised jig that fastens and locks onto his lathe. He demonstrates the entire procedure in the following pictures.

First the overall shape is roughed out of a block of East Indian rosewood shown set up for spindle turning on the lathe. By shaping first, he knows approximately how deep and long to make the grooves for the insets.

To cut the grooves, Mr. Mordaunt has fashioned a jig of 5/8-inch plywood to guide the router. *At left:* the cover has been removed from the headstock to show the index pulley inside, which has been premarked to various divisions of 360° (8, 12, 16, 24) evenly spaced around it. The artist had to create a "spacer" (a fat plywood washer) between the lathe shaft and faceplate so the cut would go far enough toward the vase's bottom.

The router is held with the base against the jig and the bit extending through the jig. Strips on each edge of the jig serve as the guide for pulling the router evenly along the cut to be made. The indexing pulley has been locked into position to prevent the vase from rotating. The jig is adjustable to various angles for a variety of shaped cuts, shown in the vases at left, opposite.

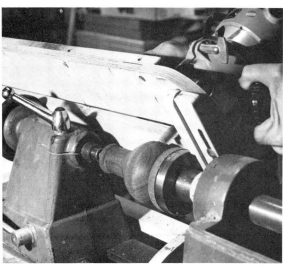

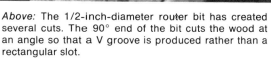

Above: The 1/2-inch-diameter router bit has created several cuts. The 90° end of the bit cuts the wood at an angle so that a V groove is produced rather than a rectangular slot.

Right: After a groove is cut, the jig continues to hold the bit perfectly perpendicular to the vase; the vase is rotated on the preset mark, and the next groove is cut.

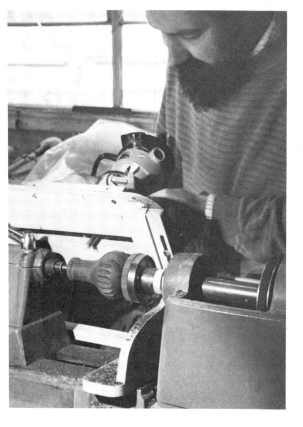

To separate the finished form from the plate, place a wood chisel on the paper separator line. Tap the top of the chisel with a mallet until the base separates from the block.

The paper will split. The paper and glue can be sanded off, and the bottom finished for a perfectly crafted base.

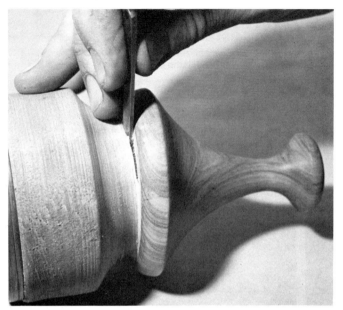

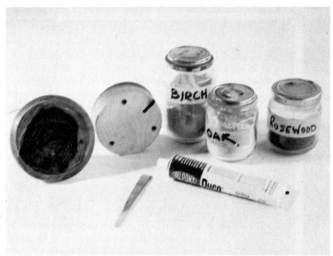

If you decide to screw the faceplate to the block as opposed to gluing a piece of parting paper between the two, sanded particles of the wood should be collected and placed in a jar.

When the block is removed, the particles of wood can be mixed with Duco cement, or other glue, to the consistency of a wood paste filler and placed in the holes, then sanded and finished.

METAL SPINNING THE CUP ON THE LATHE

Spinning metal on the lathe is a challenging use of the tool. It permits the artist to combine metals with a variety of woods, and many objects can be created. "Spinning" differs from the usual concept of lathework in that the metal is formed over a shape (called a chuck) rather than being cut away. Accessory equipment required for spinning is a ball bearing live center as well as a special type of tool rest with a fulcrum pin (seen in photos on page 81) that allows the tool to be moved evenly across the work. The tools are basically a *flat tool* and a *point tool.* The flat tool is actually round on one side and flat on the other. The round side is used to break down the metal blank against the chuck surface and the flat side is used for smoothing. The *point tool* is both a forming and finishing tool. A *beading tool* is also used to turn the rim of a metal disk into a lip or true bead. All spinning tools must be hardened steel and highly polished to avoid friction or marking the work. They may be purchased or made from 3/8-inch rod steel by heat forging, shaping, and polishing.

A back stick made of wood is also used to support the metal disk from the back during the spinning operation. It is simply a length of wood that can be made from an old broom handle and sharpened to a dull flat pointlike chisel. Its use is demonstrated in the photo series.

Any soft sheet metal can be spun. Brass is used for the punch cups shown, but one can also spin pewter, aluminum, and copper. Silver or gold may be used, but their cost makes them prohibitive. The gouges commonly used run from 16 to 22. Brass and copper require more frequent annealing than pewter or aluminum.

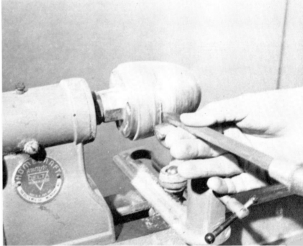

The materials required for making the brass punch cups include a chuck the shape of the finished cup, the flat tool, and the beading tool. The metal pieces show the progression of the shaping from flat disk to the finished cup.

The chuck, shaped of hardwood on the lathe, should be about an inch or so longer than the proposed spinning so there will be some space between the finished spinning and the faceplate. A metal lathed piece the same shape is also required for planishing shown on page 84, bottom left. It is cut on a metal lathe.

PREPARING THE BLANK

A 5-inch diameter circle is inscribed on the brass sheet with a compass. In all spinning, the radius of the blank should be equal to the radius of the project plus the depth of the project. The blank should form a perfect circle with a smooth edge all around.

A dot is made from the compass center of the paper template through to the brass to position the center later. Paper templates help determine how to get the most circles out of a sheet before cutting.

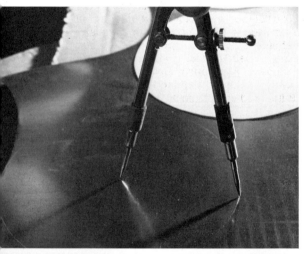

With an aviation snip, the brass is cut around the outer edge of the inscribed line. The line should remain as a guide for filing to an even, smooth edge after spinning is completed.

A dimple is dapped into the disk at the center with a 1/4-inch punch. This fits into a concave mark on the chuck and prevents the disk from slipping.

The flat disks are annealed by heating with the soft flame of an oxyacetylene torch, with a propane torch or other heat supply. Annealing softens the metal and keeps it in a working condition. It is heated to a dull red, air cooled slightly, then dipped into a pickling solution.

Pickling involves dipping the metal in a solution of 5 percent sulphuric acid/95 percent water, or a commercial pickling solution, and then rinsing in running water. Annealing must be done frequently during the spinning process because the change in molecular structure causes the metal to harden, become brittle and crack. With practice, you can detect stiffness and resistance of the metal during spinning and that calls for annealing.

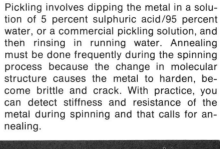

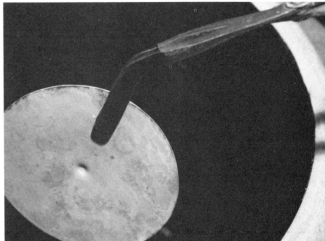

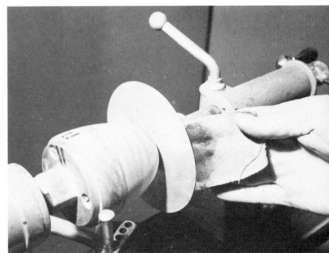

The disk is placed on the chuck on the lathe (*see next photo also*) for positioning. Observe the tool rest with the movable fulcrum pin. The ball bearing center should be brought up snugly against the disk and rotated to be sure it is properly centered. If not, the disk will get an off-center shape.

After positioning, and each time after annealing and before spinning, the outside surface should be lightly coated with grease applied with a cloth. Mr. Hunter uses a 90 weight automotive grease and just enough to allow the tool to slide over the surface without abrasion.

SPINNING INTO SHAPE

The first operation employs the flat tool placed on the tool rest between the fulcrum pin and the disk. During the spinning, observe how the fulcrum pin is moved out along with the working position to yield good leverage for the tool. Use one or two sweeping strokes off the round side of the flat tool to seat the disk against the chuck. Hold the back stick against the metal on the chuck side while the spinning disk is pressed against the opposite side. The lathe speed is about 700 RPM.

Each time the spinning begins, the tool is placed at the very center and worked down against the chuck in a back and forth movement over each area. The outer part of the metal must be kept straight like a shallow funnel and not allowed to bell out. If belling begins to occur, immediately spin the rim to a straight funnel shape.

Spinning employs two essential operations that are repeated until the required shape is achieved: crowding a small portion of the metal to the chuck surface and keeping the rest of the disk funnel shaped. The shape must be formed slowly and gradually. If you bear down and form the shape in a couple of minutes, the metal will thin and buckle.

When the metal begins to resist the shaping, it must be removed from the chuck and annealed and pickled. Here you can see the disk partially shaped in a gradual funnellike angle. When replaced on the lathe, it must be regreased.

At this point half of the cup is against the chuck. The chuck acts as the backing for the lower part, but as the tool is moved against the metal where it has not been worked to the chuck, the backing stick must be ready to place between the metal and the chuck.

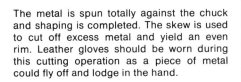

The metal is spun totally against the chuck and shaping is completed. The skew is used to cut off excess metal and yield an even rim. Leather gloves should be worn during this cutting operation as a piece of metal could fly off and lodge in the hand.

FILING AND PLANISHING

The rim edge is sharp, rough, and flat when removed from the chuck. The edge should be filed from the outside to the inside until it is dull when you run your finger along it.

The file end is covered with a piece of tape so that when you file toward the inner part of the bowl you won't mar the metal should the file slip.

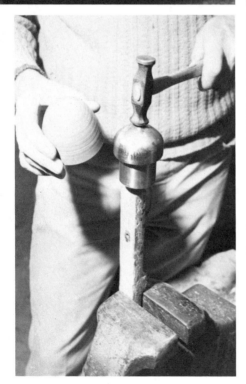

Planishing is done over a dome-shaped support (which has been turned on a metal lathe to approximate the shape of the cup) set on the end of a metal stake secured in a vise.

Planishing consists of flattening small metal areas with a hammer to remove the spinning marks and yield an interesting texture. One can leave the spinning marks if desired, or combine spinning marks and planishing.

SOLDERING THE STEM

Mr. Hunter has devised a soldering stand for easy positioning and soldering a length of 1/4-inch brass rod to the bottom of the cup. The horizontal wood shape slides up and down on the dowel at right. A screw eye at the left enables him to hold and lightly adjust the rod onto the cup which is placed on a piece of asbestos on the base piece of wood.

The brass rod is sawed to the proper length with a jeweler's saw. It is held securely by another invented apparatus made from a piece of wood clamped in the vise. The wood has a split and 1/4-inch keyhole-shaped jaw to accept the brass stem.

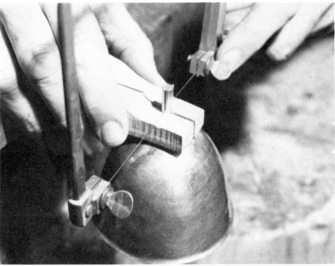

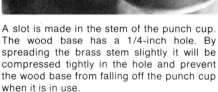

A slot is made in the stem of the punch cup. The wood base has a 1/4-inch hole. By spreading the brass stem slightly it will be compressed tightly in the hole and prevent the wood base from falling off the punch cup when it is in use.

The finished spun metal cup, now cleaned and polished, is placed in the turned wood base and the cup is complete.

Demonstration: Lawrence B. Hunter
Photo series, author

SPINDLE TURNING

The demonstrations so far have shown how to shape and bore bowls, jars, and cup bases. The basic cutting methods can be applied to achieve a variety of interesting forms for useful objects. Lawrence Hunter uses the techniques normally associated with spindle cutting but achieves a sculptural form that can be cut off at any point and perhaps drilled for a candlestick holder or a dried weed pot. When the shapes are completely severed from one another, beads can be made. With imagination, the approach can be applied to scores of objects or for embellishments such as decorative knobs, pulls, feet for other useful objects, and for jewelry.

With practice, the shapes can be made by eyeballing the turning for evenness, or one can cut a piece of heavy paper and make a template to hold against the wood and test the shaping during the turning.

Sculptural decorative forms. By Lawrence B. Hunter. Rosewood, banana, and applewoods. Spindle turning. The tall shape results when each turning is left attached. The small shapes, below, result when the individual turned forms are separated as in the bead demonstration following.

A piece of wood is roughed with the roundnose.

The wood is roughed into a round and one of the beads is beginning to be shaped.

Shaping is done with an elongated skew to cut deeply between the beads. Two beads are being turned, each will be 1 inch in diameter.

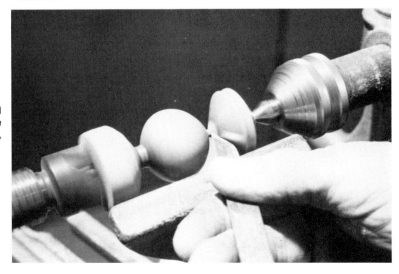

The beads are sanded on the lathe with a series of papers from coarse to fine until the bead is as smooth as desired.

An oil finish is rubbed on with the cloth. If a varnish or lacquer is desired, it can be applied in the same way.

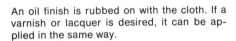

The beads are cut apart with a saw.

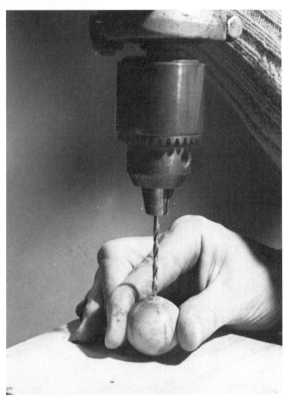

Holes for stringing are drilled.

Opposite: A string of finished wooden beads of different sizes, shapes, and woods combined with amber. By Lawrence B. Hunter.

Above: Footed serving dish by Bob Higbee made of two pieces of black walnut. 6" high, 11" diameter.

Left: An assortment of small weed pots by Bob Higbee. Six-inch diameters of dried slabs of different woods retain the shape of the log and some bark for texture. Woods include Australian teak, mesquite, apple, cork oak, manzanita. Each is about 3 1/2" high. Only the tops and bottoms are cut during turning. The pots are sealed with polyurethane and wax.

Above: Chess set and box by Tripp Carpenter. Turned chess pieces are quayacau and bay burl. The box is 5" square, and made of quayacau and rosewood.

Below: By Ada Dally. Turned cup and saucer with hand-carved cup handle. Highly figured New Zealand knitia-excelsa wood. Cup 3" high, 2 3/4" diameter. Saucer 5 1/2" diameter.

Courtesy, artist

Right: Vase by Tripp Carpenter combines an ebony wood top with an ivory base—both turned on the lathe. 4" high, 2" diameter.

Above: A pair of cleft vases by Mel Mordaunt with insets of contrasting colored and textured woods. Turned and hand-carved teak and padouk. 5" high, 4" diameter.

Courtesy, artist

Below: By Euripides Toro. A lathe-turned custom-designed stand to hold bangle bracelets. Walnut. The carved base is approximately 15" wide, 13" deep, the turnings range from 6 1/2" to 10" high.

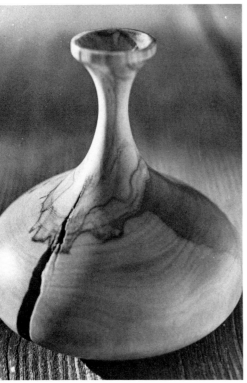

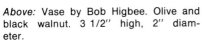

Above: Vase by Bob Higbee. Olive and black walnut. 3 1/2'' high, 2'' diameter.

Above right: Wooden weed pot by Robert Cumpston. 11'' high, 6'' diameter. All of Mr. Cumpston's pots are made from fence posts or telephone and utility poles that are old and weathered enough for the creosote to have bled out of them. After turning, they are lightly burned with a propane and special torch tip, then cleaned on a wire wheel and polished.

Right: By Euripides Toro. Turned container of oak with a black walnut base and hand-carved animal antler lid. 4 1/2'' high, 3 1/2'' diameter.

Far right: Candle holder by John Bickel. Brazilian rosewood. 8 1/4'' high, 3 1/4'' base diameter. The base and top are turned; the center section is hand carved all from one piece of wood.

Courtesy, artist

STEPHEN HOGBIN'S OVERSIZED TURNINGS

There is more than one way to turn a piece of wood using the lathe concept. Stephen Hogbin, dismayed by the size limitations of a turning on a conventional lathe, devised a turning device that would accommodate wood as large as five feet in diameter, and maybe more. The application of this turning method is only beginning to be explored by Mr. Hogbin and those who have already been stimulated and inspired by him.

Hogbin's experiments began with the usual lathe turnings, and then the concept of cutting apart the round resulted. But cutting apart a 12-inch turning only resulted in 4-by-4-inch pieces that weren't too practical. Hogbin expanded the concept and gradually visualized new ways to turn and apply the wood to art form. Mr. Hogbin realized that turnings larger than the usual board width could be accomplished only by edge gluing. He first laminated boards to one another to create a larger circumference for a turning. Then he laminated the pieces with a piece of cardboard between the edges so the turnings could be shaped, then be cut apart again and reassembled in myriad combinations. These reassemblies could be used for sculpture, for complete pieces of furniture such as tables, chairs, and so forth, and they could also be applied to objects as decorative, geometrical yet asymmetrical designs. If the sandwiched cardboard was preshaped and the wood cut down to the design, it could also serve as a template for the turning.

The result is an ability to make round turnings, cut them apart, and have them yield rectangular bowls, oblique and other shapes first unexpected, then well-planned.

The mechanics of building the unit are offered by Mr. Hogbin in the drawing on page 97. The breakdown of the differential mechanism is also given.

Basically, the wood-turning device is made from salvaged pipe, a truck's rear axle and differential turned by a one horsepower motor. Using the basic approach, one can create a similar device that is adaptable to any individual forms visualized by the woodworker.

A block of wood made of two boards has been laminated across the center with a piece of cardboard glued between (*left*). It is attached to the faceplate of the lathe, made from pipe and a truck motor. Turning proceeds in the usual faceplate scraping procedure.

After the object has been turned, it is split on the cardboard line using a wedge or mallet and chisel.

Demonstration: Stephen Hogbin
Photos, author

If desired, the board can again be fragmented into other shapes which can be applied to box tops, furniture, mirror edges, and so forth. The demonstration is with a small piece of wood, but the use of larger diameters offers additional points of departure for experimenting with the forms on a grander scale.

Top: Salad bowl, by Stephen Hogbin, of laminated woods turned and divided from a larger form.

Center: A pair of bowls by Stephen Hogbin showing the inside and outside, lathe turned and cut from a larger turning. Maple, 10″ diameter.

Left: Maple salad bowl by Stephen Hogbin. 10″ diameter.

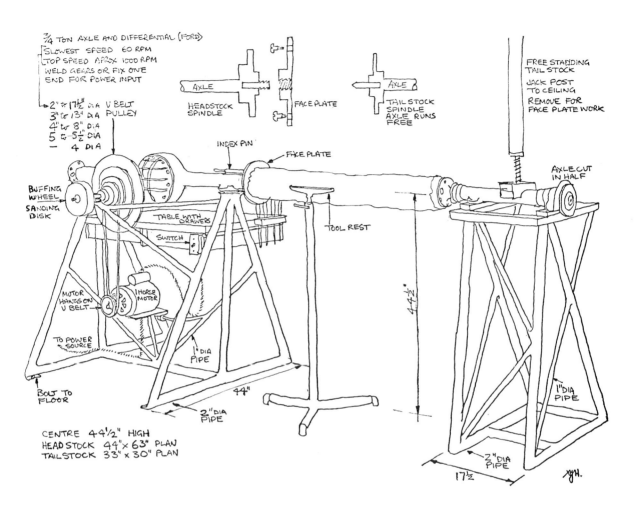

¾ TON AXLE AND DIFFERENTIAL (FORD)
SLOWEST SPEED 60 RPM
TOP SPEED APROX 1000 RPM
WELD GEARS OR FIX ONE
END FOR POWER INPUT

2" to 17½" DIA V BELT
3" to 13" DIA PULLEY
4" to 8" DIA
5 to 5½" DIA
— 4 DIA

AXLE

HEADSTOCK
SPINDLE

FACE PLATE

AXLE

TAIL STOCK
SPINDLE
AXLE RUNS
FREE

FREE STANDING
TAIL STOCK

JACK POST
TO CEILING

REMOVE FOR
FACE PLATE WORK

INDEX PIN

FACE PLATE

AXLE CUT
IN HALF

BUFFING
WHEEL

SANDING
DISK

TABLE WITH DRAWERS

SWITCH

TOOL REST

MOTOR
HANGS ON
V BELT

1 HORSE
MOTOR

TO POWER
SOURCE

BOLT TO
FLOOR

1" DIA
PIPE

2" DIA
PIPE

44"

44½"

1" DIA
PIPE

2" DIA
PIPE

17½

CENTRE 44½" HIGH
HEADSTOCK 44" x 63" PLAN
TAILSTOCK 33" x 30" PLAN

Drawing of the lathe made from pipe and
a truck motor . . .

. . . with a detail of differential assembly.
Courtesy, Stephen Hogbin

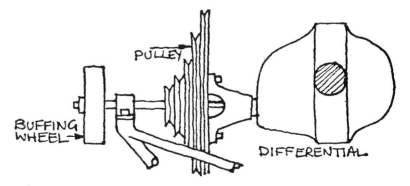

PULLEY

BUFFING
WHEEL

DIFFERENTIAL

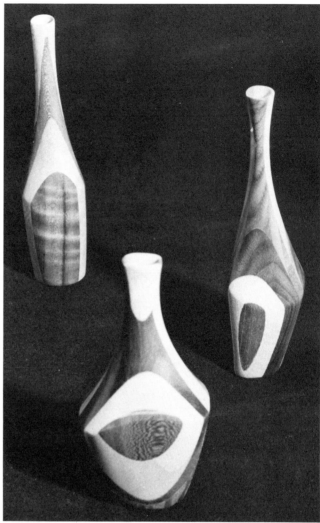

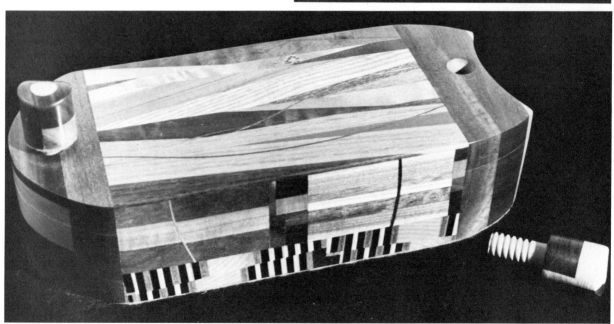

The Laminated Object

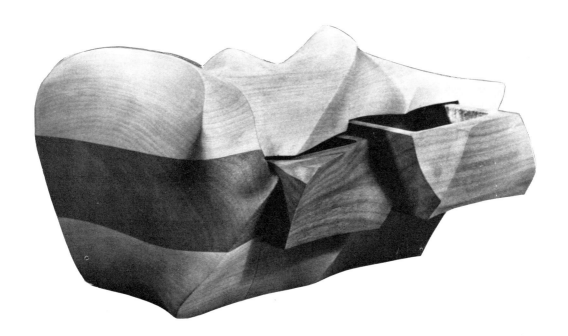

Opposite top: Weed bottles by William Jaquith Evans. A variety of laminated woods hand carved, approximately 6″ high.

Opposite below: By William Jaquith Evans. Multilaminates in several directions are made into a box with laminated screw peg fasteners. 4″ high, 10 1/2″ wide, 4 1/2″ deep.

Above: Jewelry box by Charles M. Kaplan. Three laminated layers using walnut sandwiched between cherry. Hand carved. Two sliding drawers are neatly finished so they are barely visible when the box is closed. 7″ high, 12″ wide.

Courtesy, artist

The process of building up the surface dimension of wood by layering is called laminating. It has been accomplished by woodworkers for centuries. Until the invention of glues in the middle 1700s, all laminates were dry joined. Today the application and holding power of modern adhesives makes laminating more efficient and practical than ever. Many object makers rely heavily on the use of laminating procedures for much of their work, whether it is by lathe turning, direct carving, constructing, or combinations of all techniques. They use laminating to combine different colors and textures of wood to result in a finished item with a visual and tactile appearance that is not possible using only one kind. They also laminate to yield a block of wood larger than a single board thickness.

Technically, the process of laminating involves layering two or more pieces of wood in any desired manner, either by placing the board surfaces next to each other, by gluing edges in different arrangements, by combining edge and board surfaces, or by inserting veneers between the laminates. It is also feasible to sandwich in other materials such as clear and colored sheets of acrylic and metals using adhesives that are compatible to all surfaces.

The surfaces to be laminated must be planed flat so that no gaps occur between the layers. The movement of the board's grains should be considered for expansion and shrinkage; coarse-grain woods used in damp climates, for example, may tend to separate at the glue lines. It is always good practice to assemble the boards and clamp them first without gluing to ascertain the smoothness of the surfaces and to eliminate any possible gaps. When you are satisfied with the dry clamping, then glue the surfaces and clamp adequately all around the pieces. Allow to dry thoroughly before working. Once dry, the laminates can be handled the same as a solid block of wood. Refer to the glue listing (pages 34-39) for glues available and their properties. If you plan to do quantity laminates with any given set of woods, it is wise to glue up samples using different glues to determine which give the most satisfactory results for your purposes.

Prelaminated woods of birch, plywood, and others are available from lumber dealers. These are thin layers of wood that have been glued cross-grained to one another and prepared as board for a variety of woodworking procedures. One can use the laminated boards as they are, or combine several layers for a thicker working dimension. They are also interesting when the prelaminated boards are layered in with other woods such as mahogany or walnut for differences in thickness of layers and coloration.

A variety of laminating ideas will be found in this chapter and throughout the book. They are as simple and effective as the three-layer bowls made by Charles Kaplan and as complex and jigsaw puzzlelike as the vases and other items made by William Jaquith Evans. Will Evans often uses his intricate laminates as veneers. After building up a block of various woods he will slice them veneer thin and place these veneers over a piece of inexpensive wood. With this procedure he achieves different patterns on every surface of the box and no two boxes are exactly alike because he can alter the direction of the veneer. The combinations are infinite, the procedure imaginative.

Paul Kopel develops his laminated forms by another technique. The shape is first developed in a clay model, then transposed to a laminated block of plastic foam. The foam is carved to shape and sliced the thickness of the boards to be laminated. Each slice is outlined on a board which is cut to shape. The preshaped boards are glued and clamped, resulting in a sculptural form that needs only final shaping, sanding, and finishing. This procedure permits the artist to develop sculptural form by adding on and/or carving the clay to achieve his design in the same way the sculptor works. Normally, woodworking becomes a subtractive process by which the form is attained by carving. If you carve away too much, the original form envisioned must be altered to accommodate any errors. Mr. Kopel demonstrates the procedure in the series on pages 108-111.

The procedure for building up a laminated block is demonstrated by Lawrence B. Hunter. The laminate can consist of different thicknesses of wood. A board is sliced in half on a band saw. The edges and surfaces should be put on a planer—to make them perfectly flat so they will adhere to the adjacent layers—and then sanded smooth on a belt sander.

The layers are "tested" for fit and coloration. Layers of angelique and light Philippine mahogany are interspersed with maple veneers. Dry clamp for close fit and be sure you have enough clamps.

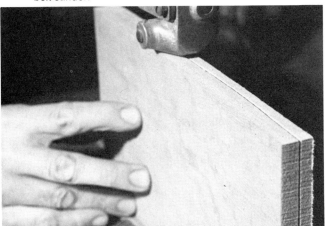

Spread glue on the layers.

Clamp up the boards. When the glue oozes, it's a good sign that the joints fit tightly. Drying time will depend on the type of glue used.

When the laminate is dry, you can cut any shape you like to achieve effects similar to those in the boxes by William Jaquith Evans.

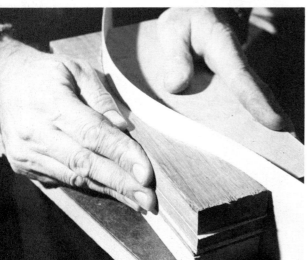

You could then insert another veneer in this way and reclamp.

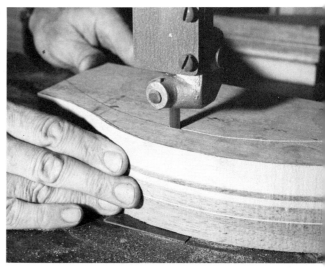

You can make as many cuts as you like to yield different shapes and laminate patterns.

Another cut reveals new possibilities.

You could place one set of cut laminates on the other and reglue and clamp. Then slice and use the slices for the surface of an object.

You can assemble the parts in any way. This could be a box if a backing and a cover were assembled to it. It could be the framed box for a mirror set onto the back and covered with another layer of wood or with laminated layers. The potentials are infinite once you begin playing with the woods and visualizing new forms.

Gumball machine. By Carol Smith. A working unit of laminated woods. A removable panel at right can be filled with gumballs. The square wood "button" is pushed in to release the balls, which fall through to four holes and troughs around the machine.

Photo, Lawrence B. Hunter

Front and back views of laminated boxes with mirrors inset. By William Jaquith Evans. The intricate patterning is accomplished by end and face laying-in of narrow and wide laminates. Sizes are approximately 5″ and 6 1/2″ high, by 2″ and 3″ wide and deep.

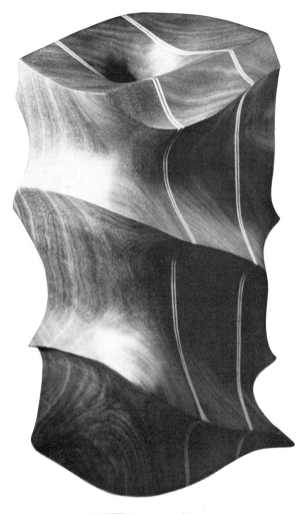

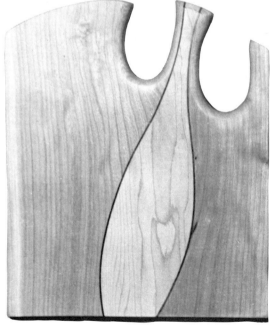

Top: Weed holder or vase by Charles M. Kaplan. Stripes are veneers laminated between walnut boards. 16″ high.

Courtesy, artist

Below: Breadboard by Wayne Raab. Cherry and maple. 12″ long, 9″ wide. Curved cuts have veneers laminated between the curves.

Right: By William Jaquith Evans. Laminated teak cabinet with locking devices. Cabinet holds a sterling silver bud vase cast from one of the artist's own laminated wood vases. 11 1/2" high, 5 1/2" wide, 5" deep.

Below: By Espenet. Redwood burl drawer fronts in a laminated walnut case. Drawers (*right*) are cut out with a band saw which provides a kerf the exact thickness of the felt lining used in and around the drawer interiors. 22" high, 4" wide, 5" deep.

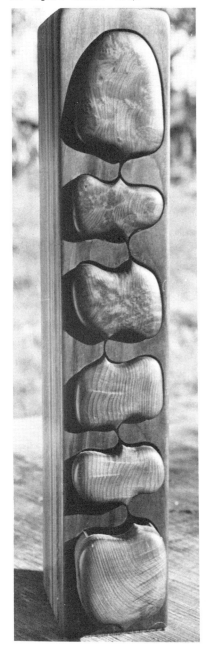

PROCEDURE FOR LAMINATING
FROM A FOAM MODEL
by PAUL S. KOPEL

Left: A drawing and clay model of a clock base show the beginning steps in Paul's work-up. Two-inch-thick foam blocks will be used for the laminate patterns. Foam slabs come in different thicknesses 1, 2, and 3″ and in large slabs 2′ X 8′ which are cut to sizes necessary for the block.

Below: The clock in plastic foam is shown after the form has been carved from the foam blocks. Tools used for shaping the foam are knives, a Surform rasp, chisels, and a hot wire for slicing the foam.

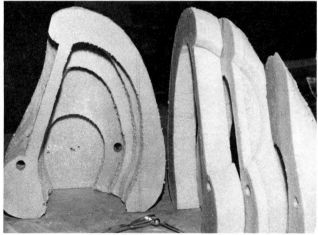

Above: The foam sections when separated: the inside has been hollowed out. Holes were drilled for registering and holding the slices together but these did not work as they were too close to the outer carved surfaces.

Left: The 2-inch-thick foam pieces are laminated by gluing with white glue or contact cement. They must dry for about a week so the glue will cure. They are shaped, then sliced to board thickness with a hot wire.

Right: The cutout wood laminates are glued.

Below: The shape of each foam piece is traced onto a board and numbered.

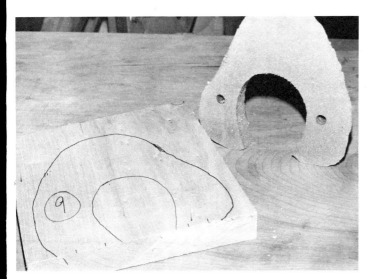

Above: One half of the form is glued and clamped at one time. Later, both halves will be clamped together.

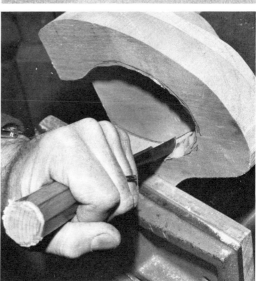

Above right: The inside shape that will hold the clock mechanism is carved out with hand chisels. A piece of wood remains for attaching the clock to the jig, which holds the face horizontal and rotates it in a circular manner under the router bit in the drill press.

A bottom view shows both halves clamped together and the cutout that will hold the clock's mechanism.

Shaping continues with a gouge and a variety of hand tools.

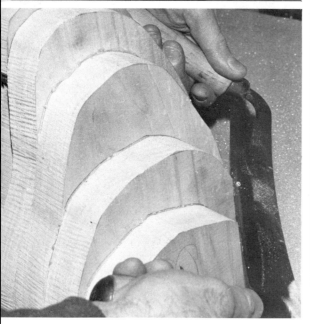

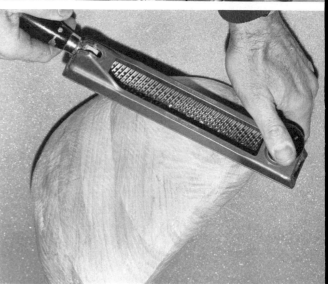

A Surform rasp continues the smoothing process.

A drawknife helps round off edges quickly.

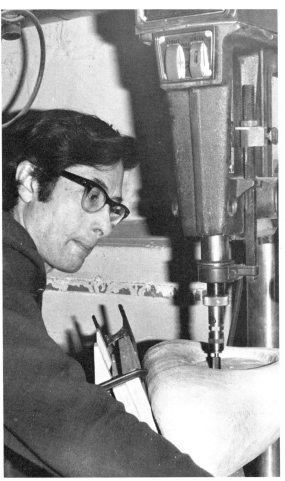

The clockface is shaped with a router attachment on a drill press.

A jig holds the clock in the drill press so it can be rotated horizontally.

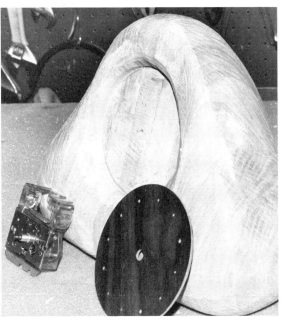

The clock as it appears before final finishing. The clockface and mechanism may be purchased ready-made.

Paul finishes the piece by hand, using several grades of sanding materials. See the following page for the finished piece.

Demonstration by Paul S. Kopel
Photos by Sally K. Davidson

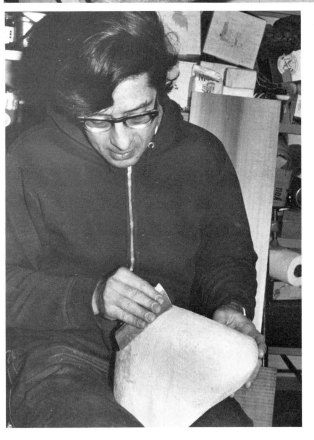

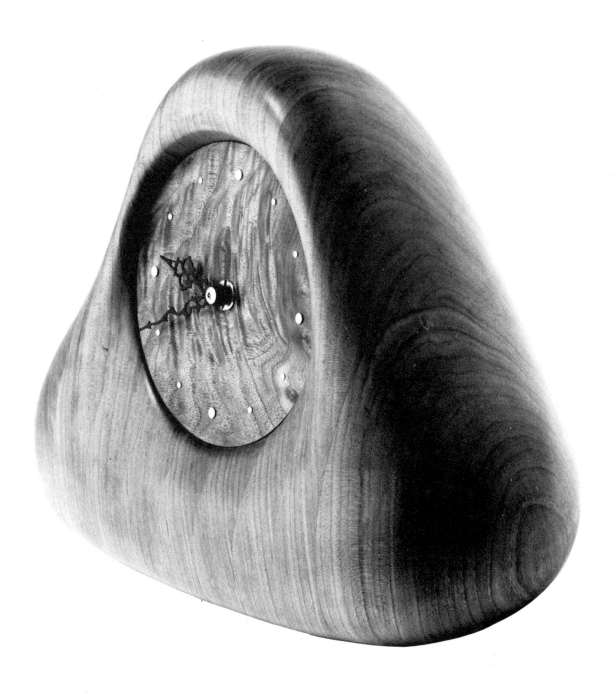

Clock by Paul S. Kopel. The face is laminated cherry and walnut with brass hour marks.
11″ high, 13″ wide, 8″ deep. Shap-
ing for all objects has been with the plastic-
foam layering technique shown in the previous series.

Collection, Dr. and Mrs. Donald Tucker
Rochester, New York
Photo, Campbell Studio

Standing mirror by Paul S. Kopel. laminated Honduras mahogany. 24″ high, 12″ diameter.

Photo, Campbell Studio

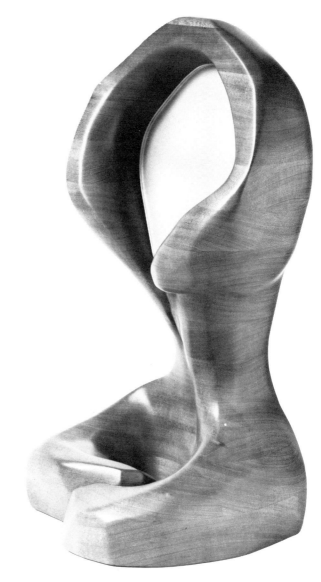

By Paul S. Kopel. Bowl of laminated Finnish birch plywood. 5″ high, 12″ wide, 6″ deep.

Collection, Mr. and Mrs. Trevor Ewell
Rochester, New York
Photo, Campbell Studio

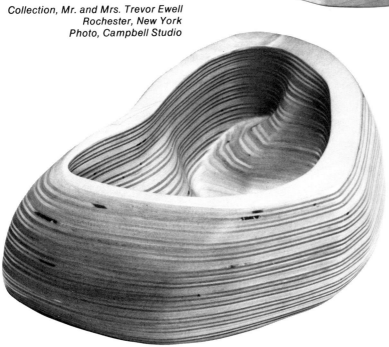

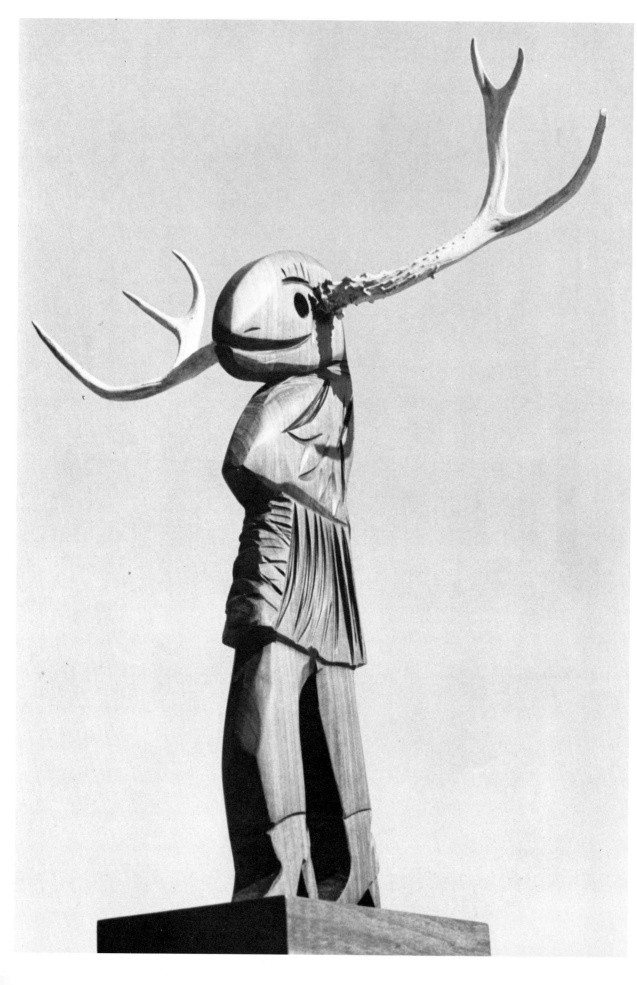

The Carved Object

Above: By Lawrence R. Jones. A laminated box with pivoting lid of East Indian rosewood, padouk, ebony, and zebrawood.
Courtesy, artist

Right: By Frank E. Cummings III. A container, lathe turned and hand carved. East Indian rosewood with buffalo fur and goat. Horsehair coiled basketry detail is on the lid. 12" high, 7" diameter.

Opposite: Deer with Antlers. By Joe Nyiri. A hat rack of hand-carved mahogany with animal horn antlers. Approximately 20" high.

Since primitive man first shaped tools and weapons from wood, the idea of carving and shaping wood for useful objects has been part of every culture. Primitive man was interested only in the form as it would function; today's object makers are interested in the form as both function and sculpture. This dual love affair with the potential of wood is apparent in the multitude and variety of examples in the following pages.

Coupled with this near-romantic involvement with wood is the sentiment that many craftsmen have about the material itself; they like to handle it, turn it, carve it, and watch the form evolve slowly, using mostly hand tools for the creative portions and power tools for roughing and finishing procedures. The forms are not those that can be achieved solely by mechanical tools; they are often free forms, organic shapes, textures, and movements that are essentially in the realm of hand-driven tools such as chisels, gouges, rasps, and files.

A great many carvers prefer to work from a log and work only from logs they themselves have found, cut, and cured. Others may be equally happy evolving their forms from cut boards, from laminated blocks, or from either logs or boards.

The ambivalent attitudes underscore the fact that there is no one way to develop a wood object. Nor does one have to be a purist. The tools used by Mexican artist José Margaro Quiroz's practiced hand are driven with utmost control and a desire for a decorative linear quality. The wood blank that is deftly carved into a bowl with a chain saw and finished with power tools by Jocko Johnson has an elegant shape, subtle curves, and beautiful finish.

The containers by Frank E. Cummings III combine hand carving with the jewelers' techniques and tools. His exciting examples utilize wood in combination with silver and ivory inlays, copper enameling, bone, horn, shells, bristles, jute, and other materials.

Jim Traynor's bottles are made from two pieces of wood glued together. First, he hollows the interior shape out of each half using a template and hand tools, so the bottle walls will be 3/8 to 1/2 inch thick. Then two halves are glued together, dried, and the exterior shape turned on a lathe. The bottles are lighter weight than if only a hole were bored through the center. The interiors are coated with several layers of sealer so they can be used as a bottle and so the object fulfills the purpose of a container.

Each artist strives to develop a design concept that is original. It may be purely imaginative or it may be derived from a source that interests him: organic, architectural, fanciful, or from the inspiration of primitive and early cultures. Once the function of the piece is established, the design is envisioned, and the work proceeds from rough sketches, detailed drawings, or the imagination. But that doesn't mean it all evolves without any problems. Given the multitude of nature's changes that permeate a piece of wood at different points in the tree's life, such as knotholes, checks and rays, summer and winter growth, and insect infiltration, the carver may have to change his direction. Larry Hunter was working with a walnut log that he had cured for two years. He had a bowl planned for the piece that would combine lathe turning and hand carving. Once he cut away the bark, a series of soft, spongy areas within the wood made it impossible to turn without chipping out large splinters. That log eventually became a beautiful hand-carved bowl with unusual shaping and texturing that he developed around the imperfections in the log.

Opposite left top: An early American food grinder meant to be only functional has sculptural qualities in its total designs as well as in the individual parts. 20″ high, 12″ diameter.

Opposite left center: A turban holder from Afghanistan with intricate hand carvings. 25″ high, 17″ diameter.

Opposite left below: A wood *garudha* from Bali has a back that opens and is a container. 12″ high, 15″ diameter.

Opposite right top: A carved wood support for a pole that holds an instrument in the Balinese orchestra. 12″ high, 6″ diameter.

Opposite right below: Wood mortar and pestle from Afghanistan is hand carved with carved surface decorations.

All objects, collection Mr. and Mrs. W. Chapman Solana Beach, California

Hand-carving procedures have changed little since the first tools were used to chip wood and the techniques are the same in every culture. Mr. José Margaro Quiroz, a master wood-carver from Mexico, demonstrates how quickly a skilled hand can manipulate razor sharp gouges and chisels to create sculptural design in the edge of a piece of hardwood. The tools are driven by both calloused hand and mallet. The wood is mahogany, but the artist carves so quickly that one would think he was cutting into butter.

Photographed at the woodworking shop
of the Muñoz Furniture Factory,
Tijuana, Mexico
Photos, author

He cuts a deep curving line with a V-shaped gouge . . .

. . . and continues to widen it near the top.

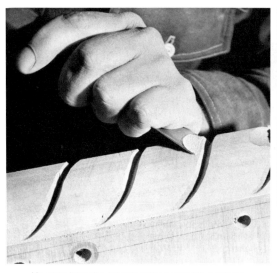

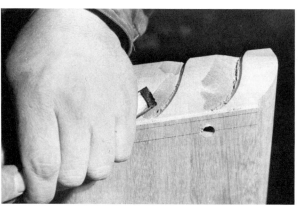

. . . and works up into the center of the groove with a flat chisel.

He cuts into the groove with a rounded chisel . . .

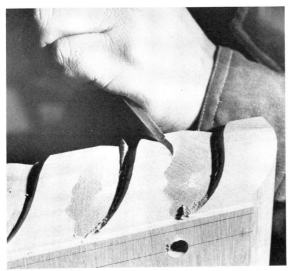

Another groove is made at about a 45° angle to
the first one.

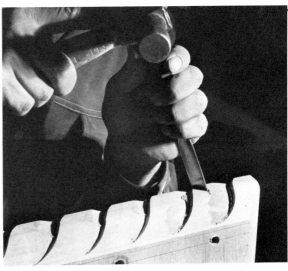

He uses the side of the hammer to drive the chisel
and penetrate the wood with a sharp, quick, slightly
curved cut.

A broad-blade curved chisel smooths off the
layers.

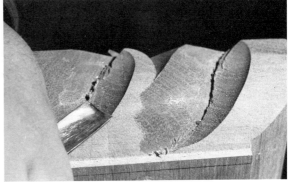

He continues to bring out the curved linear
shape . . .

. . . and gives the sweeping design a final stacca-
to note with a sharp V gouge.

ROUGH CUTTING WITH A CHAIN SAW

There are several ways to rough out a blank of wood to start a bowl or other shape using direct carving methods. The usual procedure is to chip away with wide gouges until the rough shape evolves, and then proceed to refine the shape and finish with hand and power tools. One can also drill into a blank and then chip away the remaining parts of the wood with hand tools. But Jocko Johnson finds that the use of a chain saw is, with a little practice, a quick and efficient way to hollow out the bowl.

The block is first cut to exterior shaping with a band saw. The tip of the chain saw blade is used to cut grooves which are crosscut and chipped out. Further finishing is accomplished with a rotary sanding disk placed in the drill head using an improvised valve seat grinder and working from 36 to 120 to 320 grit paper. Shaping is also done with various bits in a flexible shaft.

Jocko often fills in a hole that remains in the wood with a gemstone, using epoxy or acrylic resin to hold it in place and sanding the stone flush with the wood surface and polishing it.

Below, the evolution from pieces of rough-sawn walnut to the finished bowls are shown. Each bowl can be created in a few hours with this proce-dure which Jocko demonstrates in the following series.

The walnut blank is positioned against a supporting piece of wood, which Jocko stands on to steady.

Carving into the block begins with the tip of the gas-powered chain saw. A series of parallel lines about 3/4 of the thickness of the wood is cut across the blank.

Once all the horizontals are cut, crosscuts are made to begin chipping out the wood.

These cuts and the roughing were accomplished in about five minutes.

With the block still propped against the supporting wood, the last fragments of the interior waste wood are removed.

The shape is further refined with a sanding disk backed by a rubber pad and placed in a high speed grinder (1300 RPM).

The flexibility enables Jocko to move the sander up the gradual sloping of the bowl sides.

Grind-O-Flex sander on a Dumore flexible shaft grinder is used for additional smoothing.

Seated comfortably in a beanbag chair with
the essential-to-wear face mask, Jocko
begins to shape the bottom of the bowl with
a series of different large bits normally used
for grinding metals in automotive work.

He uses different shaped bits for taking
down the lip and side.

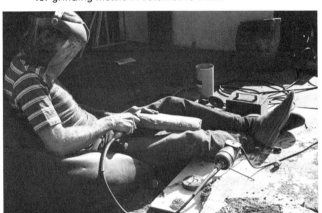

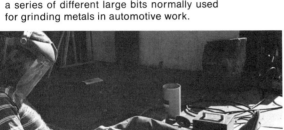

A ball-shaped rotary file in the flexible shaft
makes the indented area below the lip.

The finished walnut bowl by Jocko Johnson
is   2″   high,   12″   wide   and   3 1/2″
deep.

Demonstration, Jocko Johnson
Photos, author

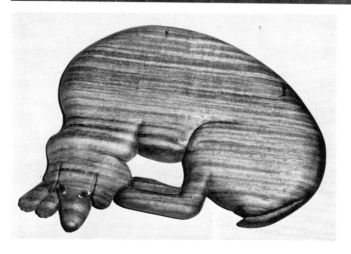

Above: Kitchen utensils by Robert Lehman. Hand- and machine-carved red oak. Overall 1/2 inch thick, 20″ high, 15″ wide.

Center: Cutting board by John Bauer of two boards, edge laminated, then carved by machine and hand in shape of bull. Maple body with eyes and nose of inlaid partridgewood. 1 1/2″ thick, 25″ long, 15″ wide.

Below: Dog-shaped cutting board by John Bauer. Genessera wood, eyes inlaid of purpleheart, ebony, and ramon wood. 2″ thick, 19″ wide, 15″ deep.

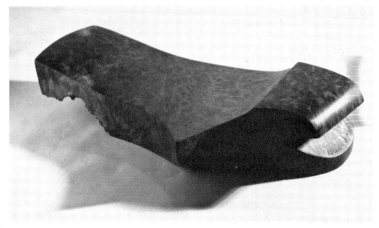

From top to bottom: By Peter Boiger. Black walnut cutting board 3 1/2'' high, 17 1/2'' wide, 9'' deep. Chopper of ebony, handles with silver pegs and a stainless steel blade. 5'' high, 8 1/2'' wide.

Meat block. By Dan L. Valenza. Walnut. 5'' high, 22'' wide, 13'' deep.

Photo, artist

Tray/cutting board by J. B. Blunk made from a redwood burl. 3'' high, 16'' wide, 7'' deep.

Cheeseboard by Tom Bendon. Laminated black walnut and zebrawood. 10'' wide, approximately 5'' deep.

Courtesy, Design 11
ACC South Central Region

By Dan L. Valenza. Tray. Walnut. 22'' diameter.

Photo, artist

Tray, *front and back views*. By J. B. Blunk, Madrone. 2'' high, 17'' wide, 10'' deep.

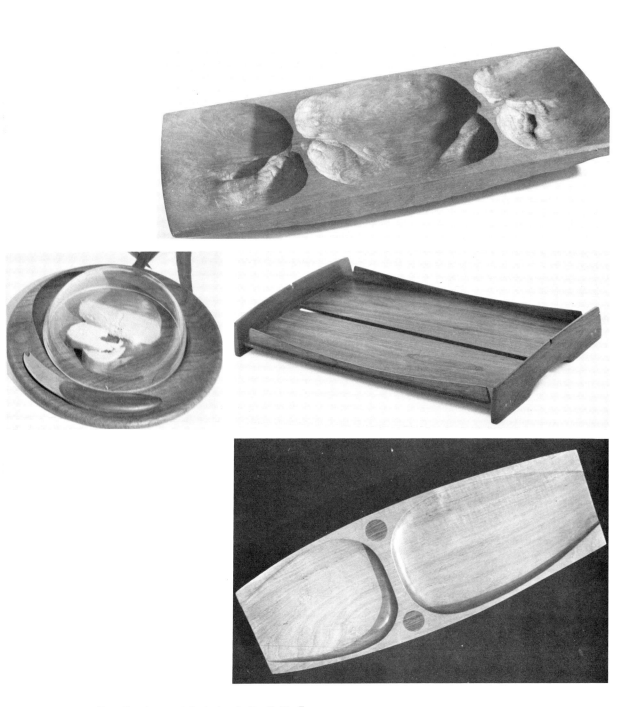

Top: Hand-carved teak bowl. By Keith E. Stephens. 2″ high, 18″ wide, 7″ deep.

Collection, Mr. and Mrs. W. Chapman Solana Beach, California

Center left: Covered dish. By Lawrence B. Hunter. Teak with acrylic plastic. Ten-inch hand-carved knife handle. Acrylic dome cover is blown with air pressure after acrylic has been softened in an oven.

Center right: Tray. By Jere Osgood. Brazilian rosewood. 2″ high, 18″ wide, 11″ deep.

Courtesy, artist

Below: Tray. By Keith E. Stephens. Teak with contrasting circle inlays. 2″ high, 23″ wide, 8 1/2″ deep.

Opposite: By Peter Boiger. Hand-carved salad servers of ebony, Brazilian rosewood, Indian rosewood, and walnut ranging from 12'' to 16'' long.

Left below: By Stephen Hogbin. Cherry wood salad servers. 12'' and 13'' long. They are designed with a lip that hooks on edge of bowl to keep them from sliding in. They may also be stored hanging on the edge of shelf as a decorative item. Maple salad bowl. 10-inch diameter.

Right below: Cherry wood ladle. Two views. By Stephen Hogbin. 13'' long.

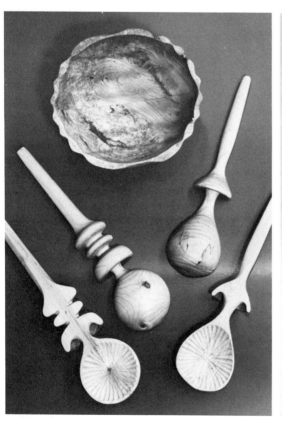

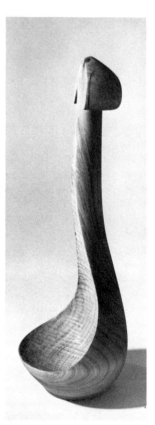

Above: By Lawrence B. Hunter. *Left to right,* Rosewood spoon 14″ long. Rosewood spatula 9″ long, teak spoon 9″ long, brass and teak ladle 7″ long, avocado bowl 5″ diameter.

Center: By Ed Zucca. Cherrywood scoop. 10″ long, 7″ wide.

Courtesy, artist

Below: By Don Boyd. Soup ladle of hand-carved applewood. 12″ long. Flour scoop of hand-carved applewood, 7″ long.

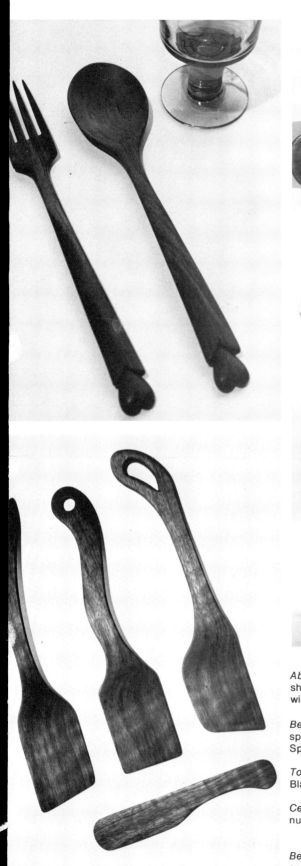

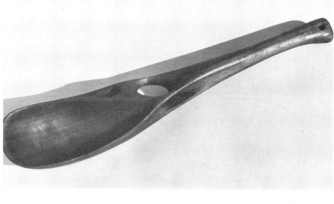

Above left: By Jay O'Rourke. Spoon and fork with heart-shape handle tip. Goncalo alves. 7 1/2'' long, 1 1/2'' wide.

Below left: By Stephen R. Johnson. Spatulas and butter spreader of shedua. Spatulas are 12'' long, 3'' wide. Spreader is 8'' long, 1 1/4'' wide.

Top right: By Jocko Johnson. Spurtle (spoon-paddle). Black walnut. 14'' long, 2 1/2'' wide.

Center right: By Dan L. Valenza. Bowl with spreader. Walnut. 3'' high, 11'' square.

Photo, artist

Below right: By Mel Mordaunt. Butter dish. Teak with acrylic. 3 1/4'' high, 4 1/2'' wide, 2 3/4'' deep.

Above: By Frank E. Cummings III. Hand-carved container of ebony with horsehair and ermine fur. 9″ high, 9″ wide, 7″ deep.

Opposite top left: By Frank E. Cummings III. Covered container of East Indian rosewood with Mylar insets, ermine fur, and quail feathers. 6 1/2″ high, 3 1/2″ diameter.

Top right: By Frank E. Cummings III. Footed, covered container of ebony with ivory inlay around foot and dentalium shells with hackle feathers. 8″ high, 3″ diameter.

Opposite below left: By Frank E. Cummings III. Ebony with ivory, hackle feathers. 5″ high, 3 1/2″ diameter.

Opposite below right: By Frank E. Cummings III. Ivory container with an ebony lid and base. Ivory inlaid around neck of lid. Gold-tipped hackle feathers around crown pick up gold color pegging in ivory. Frank works many of the details with jeweler's tools.

Above: By Jocko Johnson. Ironwood covered containers are hand carved from a roughed-out blank (*center*) and shown partially completed in foreground and fully finished in background. Detail shows interior and finish of inner lid with a piece of cork and a round of wood to keep cover from sliding.

Below left: A student at California State University, Long Beach, hand carved a hanging container with flowing lines that echo the grain of the wood.

Right: Another Long Beach student created a formed leather container with a hand-carved neckpiece.

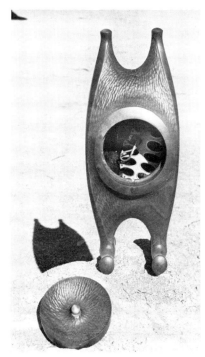

Above: By Bob Falwell. A walnut box (*closed and open views*) 6″ high, 7″ wide, 7″ deep.

Above left and center: By Sterling King. A covered container with a hand-carved hinged top that lifts to reveal a leather-covered interior.
Photographed at Triforium Galleries, San Diego, California

Below left: By Lawrence B. Hunter. Walnut container with brass fitting and silver skeleton jewelry piece inside. 15″ high, 6″ wide, 5 1/2″ deep.

By Michael Graham. A "McCallister box" of
African rosewood and Brazilian pau ferro.
18" high, 12" wide, 12" deep.
                                        Courtesy, artist

Left: Jewel container by Frank E. Cummings III. Brazilian rosewood and black hackle feathers. 12″ high, 6″ diameter.

Below left: By Lawrence R. Jones. The covered container is made of lathe-turned laminated padouk with hand-carved legs and trim of East Indian rosewood. 5 1/2″ high.
Courtesy, artist

Below right: Jewelry box by Espenet. Holly with ebony knobs. 20″ high, 4″ wide, 5″ deep.

Courtesy, artist

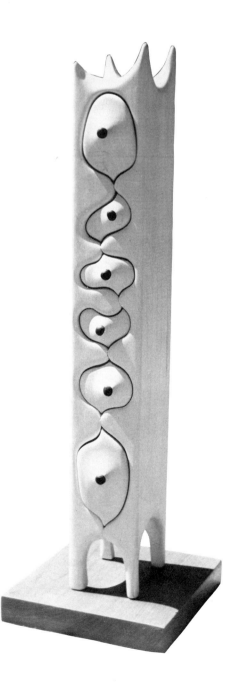

Zebrawood jewel box by Hal E. Davis (*open and closed*). There are three drawer compartments, two lidded compartments, and one pivoting double compartment. 6″ high, 18″ wide, 12″ deep.

Courtesy, artist

Above: By Fundi Kiburi. Jewel box (*closed and open*). Amaranth and zebrawood with a cocobolo catch. Compartments in lid are held closed by carved ivory turn buttons. There is an ivory inlay in the elephant's eye in front carving. Box bottom is dark glass.
Collection, Mel Mordaunt

Below: By Hal E. Davis. Figured maple jewel box with five drawers and one lidded compartment. Approximately 6″ high, 18″ wide, 12″ deep. Open and closed views. Drawers pull out with elongated handles.
Courtesy, artist

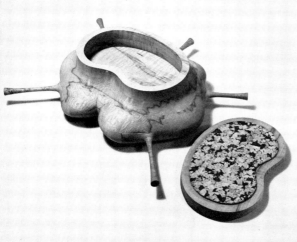

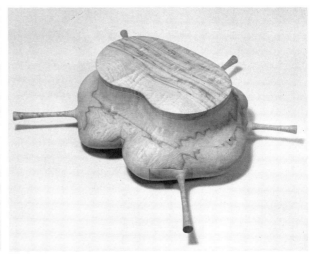

Left: By Dan L. Valenza. Piggy I jewelry chest. Laminated walnut lined in red velvet. Says Dan, "I began producing these designs as a lark and eventually was caught up in the theme: producing an amusing, if not indeed a ridiculous form, useful and perhaps a bit satirical in its stated use." The drawers have a compression in workings that produces a suck and whoosh as they are opened and shut. 6" high, 12" wide, 15" deep.

Photo, artist

Below left: Chest of East Indian rosewood by Tom Tramel. 36" high, 22" wide, 16" deep.

Photo, artist

Below right: Jewel box. By Espenet. Guatemalan gavalea wood. 24" high, 6" wide, 4" deep. Drawers pull from the front and side.

Right: By John Bickel. Walnut jewel cabinet with turned ebony pulls. 6″ high, 9″ wide, 6 1/2″ deep. The form was first made as a rectangular box and then shaped into smooth flowing curves, using gouges and mallet.

Courtesy, artist

Center: By John Bickel. Mahogany jewel cabinet with rosewood turned pulls. 6″ high, 19″ wide, 8 1/2″ deep.

Courtesy, artist

Below left and right: Walnut jewel box (*closed and open views*). By Stephen Robin. 3″ high, 12 1/2″ wide, 9″ deep.

Photographed at the Galeria del Sol, Santa Barbara, California

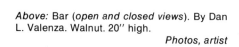

Above: Bar (*open and closed views*). By Dan L. Valenza. Walnut. 20″ high.

Photos, artist

Right: Jewel box by LeRoy Hogue. Black walnut. 8 1/2″ high, 14 1/2″ wide, 12″ deep.

Courtesy, artist

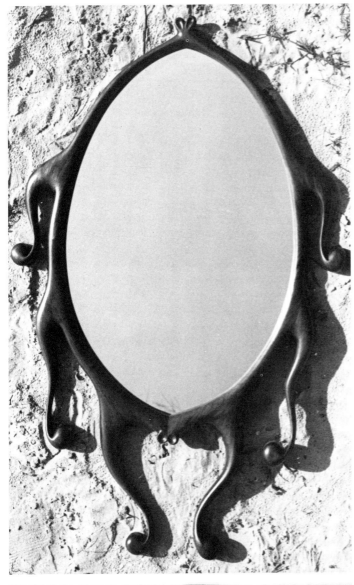

Above: Hanging mirror. By Jim Traynor. Rosewood. Approximately 26″ high, 18″ wide.

Below: Standing mirror. By Bob Daniells. Birch. 10″ high, 12″ wide, 2 1/4″ deep.

Above: Standing mirror. By Stephen R. Johnson. Padouk. 20″ high, 14″ wide.

Right: Standing mirror. By Terry Allen Smith. East Indian rosewood. 6′ high.

Photo, Tom Tramel

Opposite above left: Hand mirror by Frank E. Cummings III. Lignum vitae with dentalium shells and ermine fur at top and ivory band at top of handle. 16″ high, 8″ wide.

Opposite above center and right: By Frank E. Cummings III. Hand mirror (*front and back views*). African blackwood with ivory and dentalium shells. The ivory has been inlaid into the negative "defect" in the wood to make it a positive decorative detail. 16″ high, 8″ wide.

Opposite below: By Frank E. Cummings III. Hand mirror, comb and brush set. Brazilian rosewood, gold and silver peg inlays, javelina bristles.

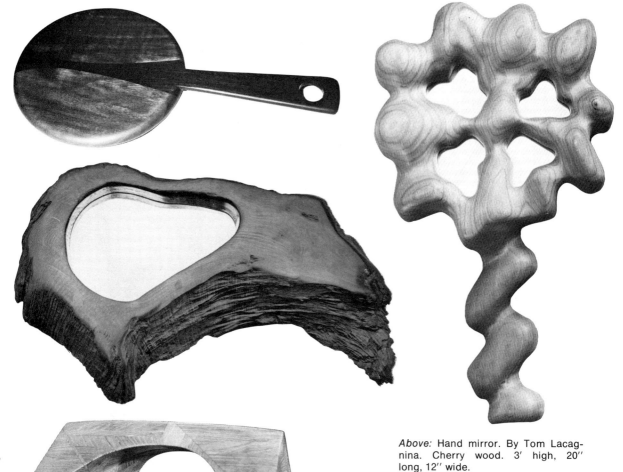

Above: Hand mirror. By Tom Lacagnina. Cherry wood. 3' high, 20" long, 12" wide.

Courtesy, artist

Left: Top to bottom
By Chris Sabin. Hand mirror. Black walnut frame with African blackwood inset and handle. 6 1/2" diameter, 12" long.

Photo, Joseph Baker

By Vince Tobaro. Hanging mirror of driftwood partially finished with carving and sanding. 2" high, 23" wide, 14" deep.

Photographed at the Tarbox Gallery, La Jolla, California

By William Jaquith Evans. Box mirror. A variety of laminated woods with mirror set on angle for viewing in the bottom of the box. 3" high, 8" wide, 4" deep.

By Sterling King. Four hanging mirrors ranging from 8" to 11" in diameter. Two with gouge-chip finish, two smooth. Right mirror has a leather piping trim set in for a raised detail.

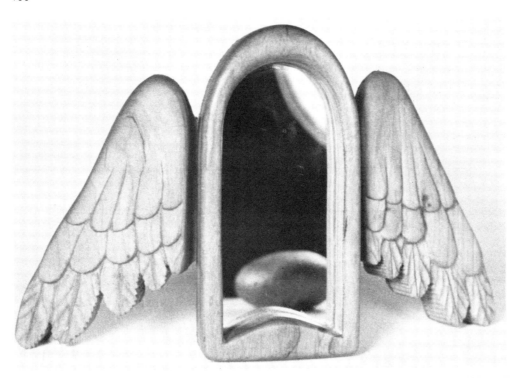

Above and center: By Elizabeth A. Tuttle. *Birdmirror.* Wings are hinged by leather backing. Cherry wood. 5'' high, 8'' wide.

Below: By Elizabeth A. Tuttle. *Birdbox.* Cherry wood. 2 1/4'' high, 12'' wide, 9'' deep. Mirror with box below. Open view.

Photos, courtesy artist

Opposite: Manzanita wood weed vase. By Bill Hunter and Harvey Holland. 10″ high, 12″ wide at base, 6″ deep. As below, one side utilizes the natural burl shape while the other is smoothly carved and finished.
Photographed at Savage's Trading Post, El Portal, California

Two views of one weed vase. By Bill Hunter and Harvey Holland. Camphorwood. 10″ high, 4″ wide, 5″ deep. The artists utilize the natural wood formation on one side and hand carve the other with a different shaping and fine finish.
Photographed at Savage's Trading Post, El Portal, California

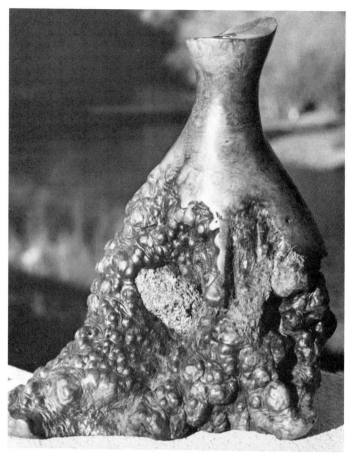

Three weed vases of manzanita wood burls by Bill Hunter and Harvey Holland. All combine the natural wood formations with some smoothing and hand finishing. Holes are drilled to accept the weed stems. *Top left:* 9″ high, 7″ wide, 5″ deep. *Below left:* 12″ high, 9″ wide, 5″ deep. *Above:* 9″ high, 7″ wide, 5″ deep.

Photographed at Savage's Trading Post, El Portal, California

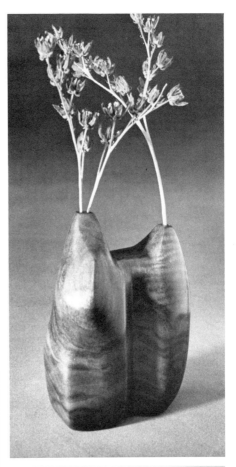

Above: Weed holder by Charles M. Kaplan. Osage orange. Some hand carving with portions of the natural bark for the exterior. 7'' high.

Courtesy, artist

Below: By Euripides Toro. Approximately 3'' high, 3'' diameter. As much of the original branch or log as possible is retained when the object is shaped and finished.

Above: By Euripides Toro. Black walnut double-necked weed vase. 4 1/4'' high, 3'' wide.

Below: Geometrically shaped diminutive weed pots of camphorwood. Sizes range from 3 1/2'' to 4 1/2'' high, and 3- to 5-inch bases. *Both, collection Mr. and Mrs. James Goodwin, Hollywood, California*

All photos on these pages are of weed pots by Doug Ayers. Front and back views of the same pots (*above left and center*) illustrate the sculptural quality and different shaping in the two faces of a piece. In all the examples, Doug combines smooth with natural and chiseled surfaces. The varied shapes attest to his personal and sensitive use of the woods that achieve an almost jewellike quality. He uses such woods as apricot, yew, osage orange, shedua, greenheart, lignum vitae, cocobolo, walnut, zebrawood, and others.

Above: By Jocko Johnson. Ironwood hookah.

Top left: By Harvey Holland and Bill Hunter. Zebrawood pipe and manzanita pipe rack.

Below: Harvey Holland and Bill Hunter. Pipe bowls of mixed woods.
*Photographed at
Savage's Trading Post,
El Portal, California*

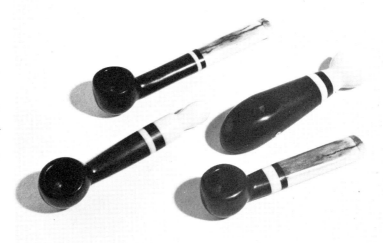

Top: Pipes by Jocko Johnson. Iron-wood.

Center: By Joel Rich. Intricately carved brierwood pipes.
Courtesy, artist

Below: By Bill Horgos. Four pipes combining different kinds of woods.

CANES AND STAFFS

Top: Staff with fantasy carvings of castles. By Jim Pasek. In addition to their function as a walking aid, the staff's castle tops are removable and hold a small vial for medical aids or paraphernalia. Staffs are 64″ long with curved tops of exotic woods such as bubinga, cedar, purpleheart combined with oak and rosewoods. The shafts are usually a hardwood such as oak or ebony for strength.

Below left: A screw-off top reveals a place for a small glass vial within. By Jim **Pasek.**

Below right: Walking cane by Jim Pasek has a bird head of cherry wood with rosewood, maple, oak bands and pegs, and an oak and ebony shaft. Carved head is 3″ high, 5″ wide, 1 3/4″ deep.

Opposite: A collection of canes antique and modern. *Left to right:* Spanish cane with figures of Christ. English guild figure. Alligators carved on head and handle, from Africa. From Spain, an intricately carved Moorish design with a bird on top. An American cane of maple from about 1880. A contemporary example in parambuke wood with ivory pegs from Durban, South Africa. All about 36″ long.

Collection, Dr. N. H. Gladstone,
Beverly Hills, California

MISCELLANEOUS OBJECTS

The range of useful objects illustrated in this chapter is varied. While many fall into specific categories such as trays, weed pots, miniatures, and so forth, others do not. Therefore, the following pages offer a variety of examples that you may or may not have thought of creating. There may be those you have not associated with a "handmade sculptural-functional object." You will find examples of buttons, buckles, hair ornaments, and weavers' tools, puzzles, doors, and door handles. Most unusual and magnificently crafted are the crematorial urns by Norm Tornheim.

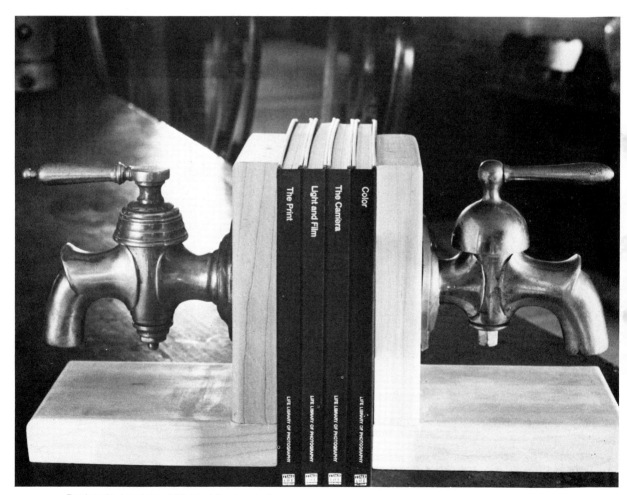

Bookends by John Hilbert. Mixed woods.
12″ high.
Collection, Mr. and Mrs. Joseph Kraft,
Courtesy, Irene Towbin, New York

Puzzle. By Marta Pan. Laminated woods.
8″ high.

Courtesy, artist

Weavers' and crocheters' tools are often handmade. The objects are always held and felt by the hands, and craftspeople working in any medium are receptive to a well-shaped object. *Above and center:* Beaters and crochet hooks in different sizes and of assorted woods.

Courtesy, "Spin it-Weave it" Studios, El Cajon, California

Above right: By Jay O'Rourke. Pronged hair-sticks of greenheart and goncalo alves woods. They vary in height from 6 to 8 1/4'' and from 3/4-inch to 2-inch width.

Right: By Walter Easton. Drop spindles for weaving are birch and cherry wood. 14'' long, 4'' diameter. Lathe turned with hand-carved details.

Courtesy, artist

The finished inlaid veneer (*left*) is ready to be glued to the box top. Spread glue on the box cover.

Then spread glue on the inlay.

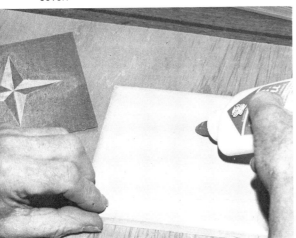

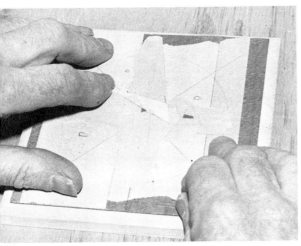

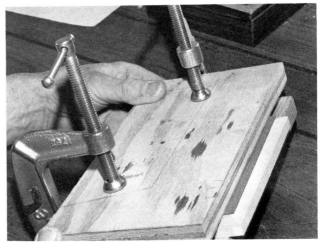

Place the inlay upside down on the box (notice that the tapes are still in place).

Adhere to box top with clamps. Use two pieces of scrap wood larger than the top and sandwich the box top between them to prevent clamps from marking up box and veneer. Let dry thoroughly.

The tape is peeled gently from the box. If the veneer overlaps the edge, trim it down carefully all around.

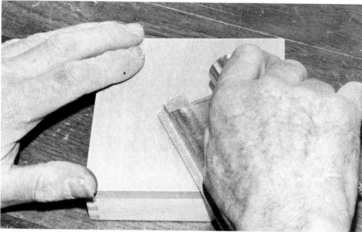

The entire box should be sanded, using first medium and then fine sandpapers. Electric sanding tools may be used also, very carefully, so as not to disturb the inlay.

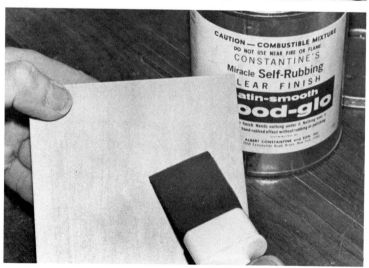

The box is varnished and finished by rubbing with steel wool. It may be waxed, if desired.

*Demonstrations by
William E. Brewerton,
Photos by Sally K. Davidson*

THE SAW METHOD

Using a fine jeweler's saw, or a special blade for marquetry on a jigsaw, several layers of veneer can be cut simultaneously. This has the effect of "production" but still retains the handmade quality because the use of different color veneers yields an infinite range of color-in-design possibilities. Although the basic design remains the same, no two veneers need be exactly alike because of the interchange of coloring. Too thick a saw will result in too much kerf, or gap, between the inlay and the background shape. Use a blade as small as a #8 in a jeweler's saw.

When using a saw, the pieces must be taped as with the knife. If more than one veneer is to be cut simultaneously (up to 10 is about the limit), fasten the veneers to one another by coating each piece (except the top) with rubber cement on the tapes (not on the woods). Place pieces of tape around the edges of the layers to keep them secure and place them under a weight until the rubber cement is dry.

To start the holes in the background veneer use a very thin electric drill bit or a needle slightly larger than the saw blade. Make a tiny hole at a corner of each portion of the pattern. The saw blade is pushed through this starting hole and cutting proceeds.

A V-shaped wooden slotted board clamped to a table makes an efficient surface for holding the veneer and allowing the saw to wiggle around the holes. After the pieces are cut, push them out with a pointed object.

Keep the veneer cutouts of each shape in a different container to make it easier to find them when you are ready to inlay. It's a good idea to number above each hole in the background and place each inlay of the corresponding shape in a container with that number.

When multiple pieces of veneers are cut, often the fit of the inlay into the hole is not as accurate as when only one sheet is cut with a knife. If spaces exist between the inlay and the background, these can be filled in with sanded particles of the wood mixed with white glue to make a wood putty consistency.

When you separate the sandwiched veneers that have been held with rubber cement and tape, remove any sticky residue by peeling it off or rubbing lightly with a rag moistened with turpentine. The tape that holds the inlay is removed only *after* the veneer is assembled on the object. Assembling and finishing are accomplished in the same way as in the preceding series on marquetry.

All demonstrations by William E. Brewerton,
Photos, Sally K. Davidson

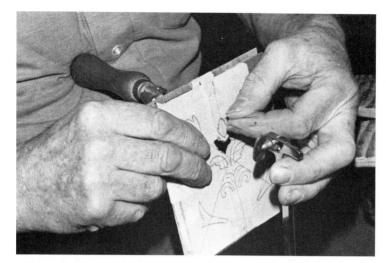

A jeweler's saw, or a fretsaw, is used with the teeth of the blade downward toward the handle. One end of the blade is placed in the saw jaw; the blade is then pushed through the tiny hole made in the veneer and the other end tightened into the other jaw of the saw. The blade must be taut.

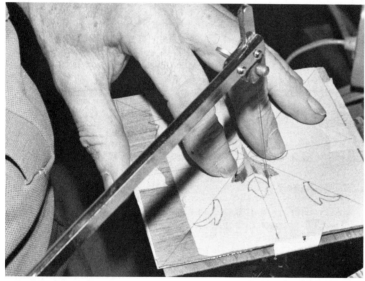

The saw blade is manipulated around the lines of the pattern. The pieces are then pushed out with a pointed tool.

Inlays cut from one color veneer are placed in the background veneer of a contrasting color. Edges are glued in and any kerf, or gaps, are filled in with sawdust mixed with glue.

Above: Small hutch by William E. Brewerton. Marquetry.

Below: Music box by William E. Brewerton. Marquetry.
Photos, Sally K. Davidson

Traditional marquetry is time consuming and a labor of love. Even if one attempts to reproduce the same design several times, each piece is still individually handcrafted. William Jaquith Evans, himself well versed in marquetry techniques, wanted the beauty of inlaid veneer woods combined with a process that would make the production of the items economical enough to market at craft shows. He insets dowels into blocks of wood using the same principles that Milon Hutchinson demonstrated in his decorative pegged bowls (chapter 3). Will, however, inserts long pegs or dowels into the block and then slices the block into thin veneers or thicker slices depending upon the object to be made. For the earrings, below, he combines a unique approach to laminating with doweling for intricate inlay effects. The mirrors and cigarette holders (page 199) were made of thicker slices of the woods. He demonstrates the doweling technique.

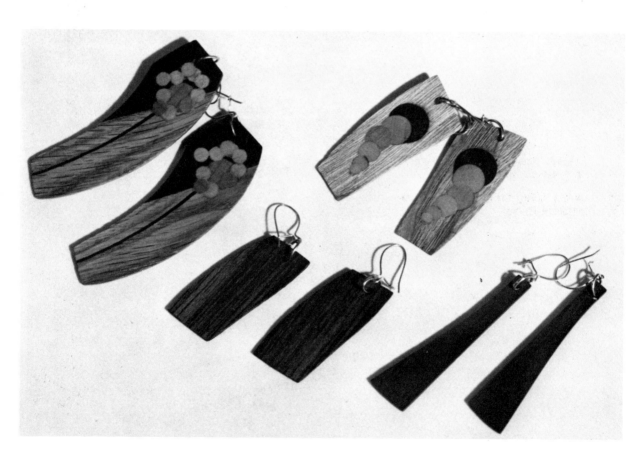

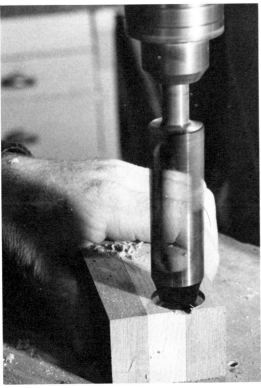

Left: First a block of ash and mahogany is laminated. A 5/8-inch-diameter plug is cut with the laminate line across the center to yield a two color plug.

Below: Several plugs are cut out of the block and the laminate line may appear randomly across any portion of the surface.

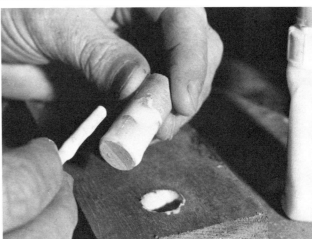

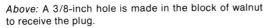

Above: A 3/8-inch hole is made in the block of walnut to receive the plug.

Right center and below: The plug is glued. Glue is applied with a thinner dowel and the plug placed in the walnut. If the plug needs coaxing to force it into the hole, place another length of dowel in the drill chuck and use the pressure of the machine to push the plug into the walnut. Dry thoroughly.

Opposite: By William Jaquith Evans. Earrings, plain and inlaid.

When the first plug is dry, a second hole, 1/2
inch in diameter is drilled. A 1/2-inch plug of
ash has been cut and placed in the second
hole and a third, 3/8-inch hole is drilled and
filled with a walnut plug cut from a grain pattern that differs from the block.

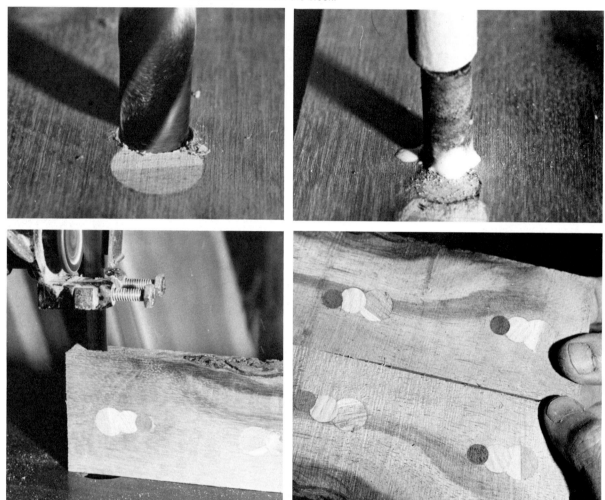

When all plugs are dried in the board (here
two sets have been inlaid), the board is
placed on the band saw and sliced in half
and then in half again and again until a multiple number of thin slices is created. The
slices are reclamped together and the earring shapes are cut out.

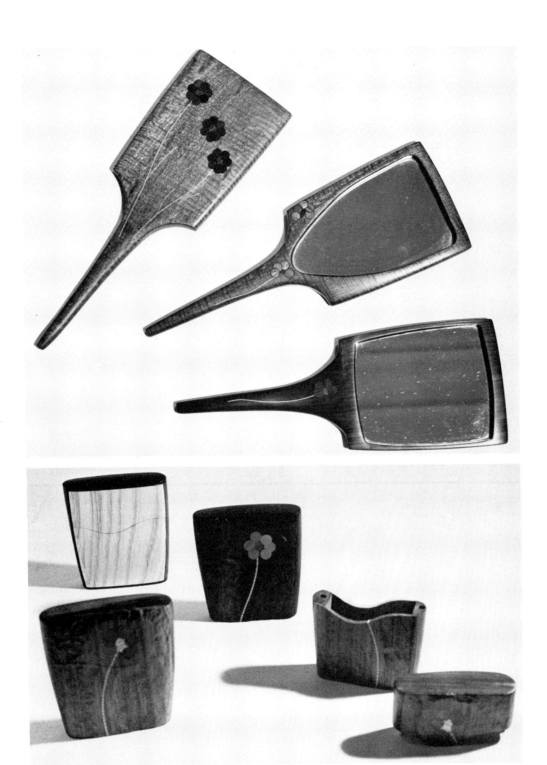

Above: Vanity mirrors by William Jaquith Evans. Brazilian rosewood and fiddleback mahogany. Floral patterns are made with a series of overlapped plugs and with veneers laminated in the wood block for stems. Inlay appears on fronts and backs of mirrors.

Below: By William Jaquith Evans. Cigarette or playing card boxes. 4″ high, 3 1/2″ wide. Inlaid panels used for fronts and backs with sides added and ends rounded.

Above: By Keith E. Stephens. Rosewood bowl with ivory inlay at tip of handle. 14″ wide, 3″ deep.

Above left: By John Bauer. A wall cabinet of madrone and cypress with a hand-sculptured door and inlay. The background oval is teak, the moon is bone, the coat is rosewood, the chicken, feet, and moustache are ebony, and the hat and shirt are boxwood. Other details are purpleheart and amaranth. 23 1/2″ high, 19″ wide, 6″ deep.

Below: By John Bauer. Wall hanging knife holders inlaid with teak, rosewood, madrone, and other woods. The left holder has a cherry front and acacia back. The right one is walnut and acacia.

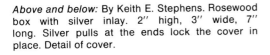

Above and below: By Keith E. Stephens. Rosewood box with silver inlay. 2″ high, 3″ wide, 7″ long. Silver pulls at the ends lock the cover in place. Detail of cover.

Above: Mirror by Robert Salleroli. Dowels inlaid in a frame are used so that the length of the dowels form a pattern and slanted line; the round end cuts form a counterpoint and appear in three different diameters. 51 1/2″ high, 32″ wide.

Courtesy, artist

Below: By Al Miele. Marquetry. Jewelry box with secret compartment. 3″ high, 12″ wide, 8″ deep. English walnut box with inlay of ebony, tulipwood, and brass.

Courtesy, artist

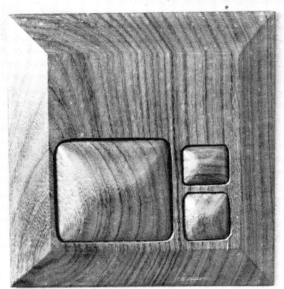

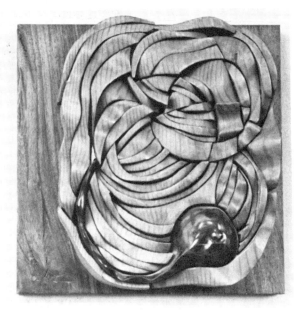

Ideas for wood inlays for relief patterning.
*Photographed at California
State University, Northridge*

Opposite: By Christopher Sabin. Cutting
board. Curly swamp maple with African
blackwood inlay. 18″ high, 8″ wide.
Photo, Fred Weiss

Letter stand by Conway Pierson. Birch, hickory, walnut, and bronze castings with a ceramic pot. 24″ high, 20″ wide, 20″ deep. Hand-carved wood parts are assembled using refinished wheels from fishnet hoops. The stand arm is a snath, the handle of a scythe.

Courtesy, artist

7 Constructing and Carving

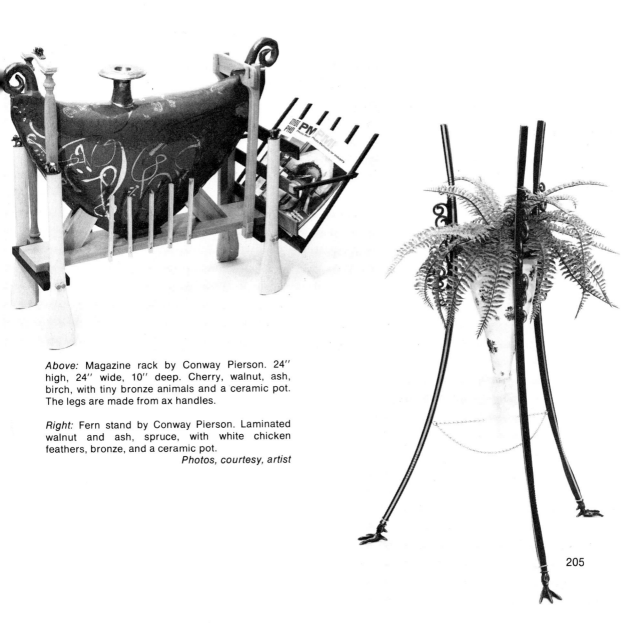

Above: Magazine rack by Conway Pierson. 24″ high, 24″ wide, 10″ deep. Cherry, walnut, ash, birch, with tiny bronze animals and a ceramic pot. The legs are made from ax handles.

Right: Fern stand by Conway Pierson. Laminated walnut and ash, spruce, with white chicken feathers, bronze, and a ceramic pot.

Photos, courtesy, artist

Joinery, the practice of uniting or combining pieces of wood to extend the dimension in length, thickness, or width, or to change direction, has been used by woodworkers for countless years. Until the use of glue, only joinery was used for butting together edges of wood, mitering corners, pegging, and so forth.

Small objects do not receive the stress and wear qualities of heavier wood items such as furniture, floors, and ships, but the application of basic joints to create boxes, jewelry cabinets, musical instruments, toys, and other useful accessories is an important part of the craftsman's working vocabulary. A joint is often a visual as well as functional detail. For example, a box corner could be made by butting two pieces of wood but a dovetail joint will add measurably to the visual quality of the box. The joint may be made from a different wood so it will contrast with the color of the basic structural wood.

There are about a dozen much-used woodworking joints, and each has several variations. An assortment of joints used in small objects is pictured on the following pages. These can be made by observing the drawings and cutting the parts to shape with saw and chisels. Directions for creating compound and more complex joints can be found in handyman's magazines and in carpentry and woodworking books listed in the bibliography.

Practically all joints may be reinforced with glues and/or fasteners such as nails, screws, pins, wedges, splints, dowels, corrugated fasteners, and other hardware, depending upon the stress that will be put on the joint.

The stress that a joint will receive will usually determine how it will be made. The contents of a drawer resist the effort you apply when you pull the drawer out. All the strain is on the joint connecting the drawer front to the sides and, therefore, dovetails are usually used. The interlocking feature resists the strain and will continue to do so even if the glue dries out. A pegged joint will do the same job and is easier to make than the dovetail.

The strength of any joint depends largely on the accuracy of the fit to the joining members, the quality of the glue, and the efficiency with which the pieces have been glued and clamped. Other factors that affect the strength of the joint are the porosity of the woods being joined, how the glue adheres to the fibers, and the degree of movement in the wood, that is: how much it swells and contracts under varying humidity conditions. The standard of workmanship is, of course, of utmost importance.

Intricate joints are time consuming and, if an object is made for a selling market, it is more economical timewise to use the simpler joints. You may want to make the intricate joints for the sake of craftsmanship and to enhance the appeal of the object. All the factors must be weighed when you design and create the object.

In addition to usual joinery methods, many of the following examples employ inventive solutions for connecting parts such as handmade hinges, movable joints, hand-turned wood screws, and others. Often the joinery and construction have been so perfectly concealed that the object appears to have been hand carved from a solid piece of wood. In a few examples, such as musical instruments, the objects are not constructed, only carved and these have been placed here for the sake of organization rather than method. The two procedures, constructing and carving, are so compatible that placement of some items in one chapter rather than another was an arbitrary selection.

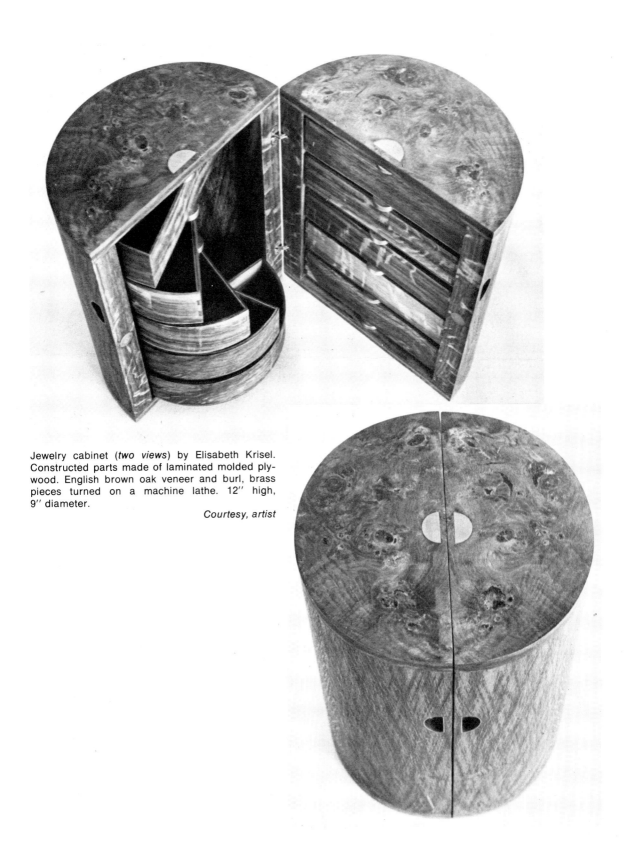

Jewelry cabinet (*two views*) by Elisabeth Krisel. Constructed parts made of laminated molded plywood. English brown oak veneer and burl, brass pieces turned on a machine lathe. 12'' high, 9'' diameter.

Courtesy, artist

SIMPLE JOINTS

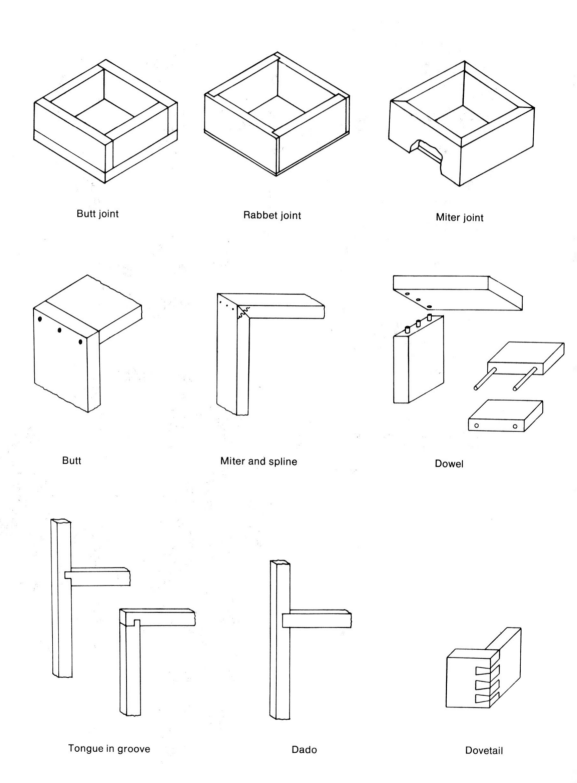

Butt joint

Rabbet joint

Miter joint

Butt

Miter and spline

Dowel

Tongue in groove

Dado

Dovetail

APPLICATION OF JOINTS IN DIFFERENT COLORED WOODS   *Examples by Lawrence B. Hunter*

Half lapped and cross lapped

Dado

Dovetail

Wedge peggings

Box joint

Blocks of wood, intricately carved with geometric patterns, can be used any way the imagination dictates. The squares can be used for box tops, assembled for tables, doors, and applied on other objects. Milon Hutchinson shares his methods for carving the blocks using the radial arm saw with the indexing concept already shown in chapter 3. He places the block on the indexer and makes cuts in many directions. "You have to play around with it," says Milon, "until you get the feel of what the saw will do at different progressive settings." Linear designs can be combined with circular forms made on the drill press with circle cutters or with router cuts.

Left: The block has a hole in the back that fits on a peg to hold it tightly to the indexing wheel. A stopboard is also on the holding surface.

Below: The first cut is made.

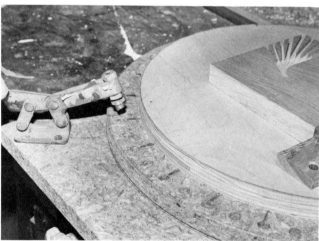

The index is turned one preset notch for each cut and for as many cuts as desired on one side of the block. The lever fits into pre-bored holes in a circle. By changing the number of holes between cuts, different designs result.

When the block is turned and cut from the other side, the geometric design in the center becomes apparent.

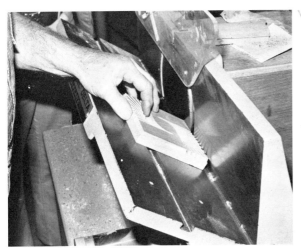

Edges are safely and easily beveled on a Rockwell uniplane which can make micrometerlike cuts any angle from 0° to 45°.

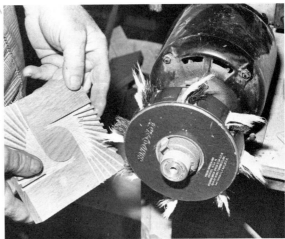

Shredded sandpaper in a Sand-o-Flex grinding wheel makes quick work of smoothing the grooves.

A small assortment of the myriad possibilities of carving in this manner.
Demonstration by Milon Hutchinson
Photos, author

Spinning wheel by Bob Daniells. Hand carved and constructed. Red oak and walnut. 36" high, 36" wide, 14" deep.

Detail at right: All parts can be dismantled. Metal spokes are held to the wheels by pegs; all gears, nuts, axles, and wood parts are hand carved and lathe turned.

Above: Hand-carved clock mechanism by John Gaughan (*detail of large grandfather clock*). Brazilian rosewood. The wood gears perform functionally but their interacting parts create a kinetic sculptural motion.

Right: CLOCK III (*detail*). A handcrafted clock by Lawrence B. Hunter. Laminated and carved cherry wood. The concept of the hand-carved escapement suggests a fanciful animal whose head moves slowly, perpetually, back and forth.

Top: By Tom Bendon. Pau ferro clock case. 8" high. Electronics by Ed Muns.

Courtesy, Tom Bendon

Below: Two clocks by Jere Osgood for wall or desk use. Battery powered. The larger one is made of goncalo alves with a maple face. 11" high, 9 1/2" wide, 2 3/4" deep. The smaller clock has a cherry wood case with a figured maple and walnut face.

Courtesy, artist

Top: By Tom Bendon. Pau ferro clock case. 8" high. Electronics by Ed Muns.

Courtesy, Tom Bendon

Below: By John Gaughan. Brazilian rosewood with two chrome balls that operate on a magnetic field principle. 2 1/4" high, 8 1/4" square.

Top: Fantasy radio cabinet of laminated woods by Wilfred Malmlund. 34″ high, 18″ wide, 12″ deep.

Below: Clock radio by John Bickel. American black walnut with rosewood knobs. 4 1/2″ high, 12 1/2″ wide, 4 1/2″ deep. The cabinet was constructed as a rectangular box, then shaped with a band saw, gouges, and mallet.

Courtesy, artist

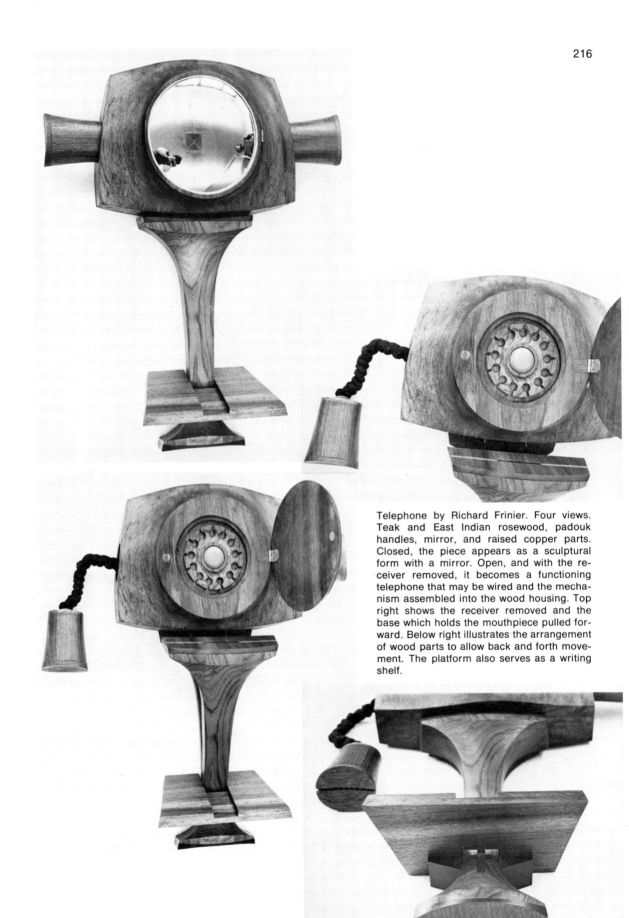

Telephone by Richard Frinier. Four views. Teak and East Indian rosewood, padouk handles, mirror, and raised copper parts. Closed, the piece appears as a sculptural form with a mirror. Open, and with the receiver removed, it becomes a functioning telephone that may be wired and the mechanism assembled into the wood housing. Top right shows the receiver removed and the base which holds the mouthpiece pulled forward. Below right illustrates the arrangement of wood parts to allow back and forth movement. The platform also serves as a writing shelf.

Another telephone cabinet by Richard Frinier. Closed and open views. East Indian and Brazilian rosewood with formed leather center at the mouthpiece area. Horsehair hangs at bottom of removable part that becomes the receiver. 24" high, 8 1/2" wide, 4" deep.

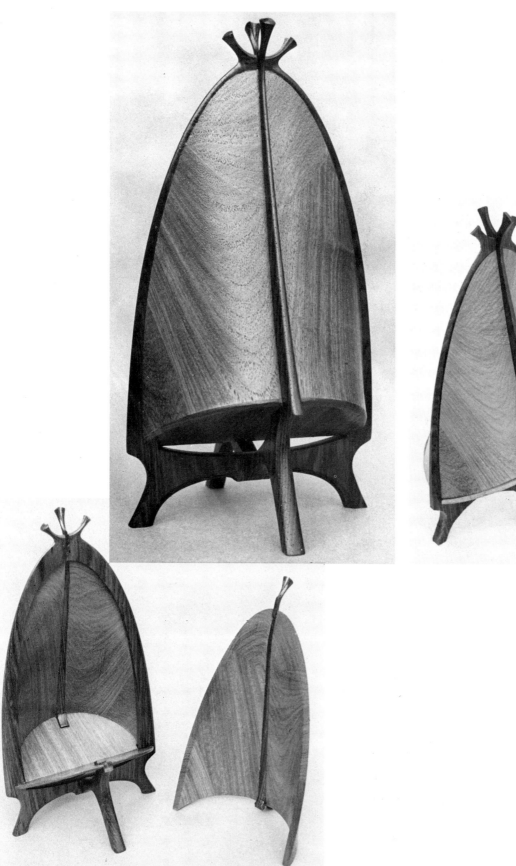

Opposite: Covered container by Lawrence R. Jones. Three views. Nara wood body with Brazilian rosewood legs. Some lathe-turned parts with hand-carved details and legs. 13" high, 6" wide.

Courtesy, artist

Covered container by Lawrence R. Jones. Brazilian rosewood, with bronze cover. 13" high, 6" wide.

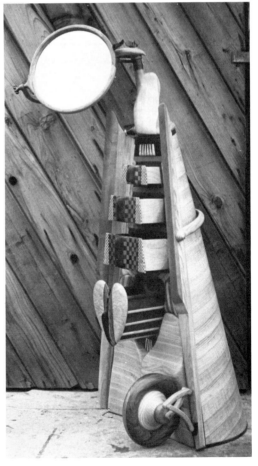

By Robert Strini. A jewelry box with drawers and adjustable mirror on a swinging bar. 5 1/2' high. A variety of laminated woods with a bird's-eye maple heart-shaped drawer. Open and closed views and details.

Photos, artist

By Bob Daniells. Jewelry chest of red oak and walnut. 27″ high, 7″ wide, 7″ deep. Drawers pull out (*right*). Because the narrower dimension at the top makes the drawers difficult to get into, they are hinged to open sideways.

Above (closed and open views): Jewelry box by George Gordon. Cherry with the drawer fronts of cherry burl veneer. The drawer handles are turned ebony. 14″ high, 25″ wide, 10 1/2″ deep.
Collection, Mrs. Jody Todd
Rochester, New York
Photos, artist

Left: Jewelry cabinet by Hal Ross. Teak with a hidden compartment. 17 1/4″ high, 8″ wide, 8 1/2″ deep.

Photo, artist

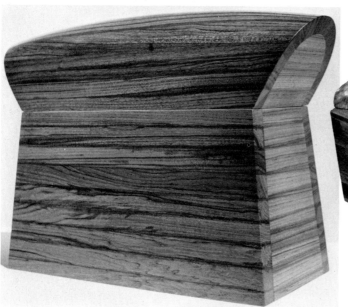

Above: By Wayne Raab. Black walnut box dovetailed and carved. 5'' high, 10'' wide, 4'' deep.

Courtesy, artist

Above left: ANNIVERSARY PIECE by Lyle Laske. Of teak and ebony with a Sarna bell within. 10 1/2'' high, 15'' wide, 6'' deep.

Collection, Francine Laske
Courtesy, artist

Center left: By Lyle Laske. Wedding chest. Teak. 14'' high, 20'' wide, 8'' deep.
Collection, Mr. and Mrs. Sol Koppel
Courtesy, artist

Below left: By William Jaquith Evans. Laminated and constructed jewelry box with pegged inlays. 6 1/2'' high, 8'' wide, 5'' deep.

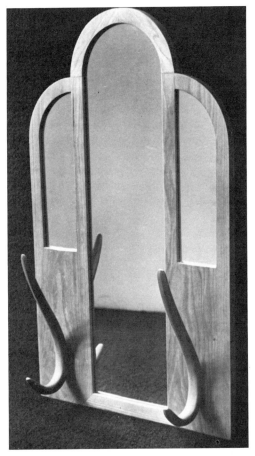

Above left: By Mark Paulson. Jewelry cabinet. Cherry with maple panels. 28″ high, 18″ wide.

Above right: By Mark Paulson. Hat rack with mirrors. Cherry. 22″ high, 14″ wide.

Below (open and closed views): By Mark Paulson. Collector's box that holds a piece of a shell. Cherry and vermilion. 8″ high, 8″ wide.

All photos, courtesy artist

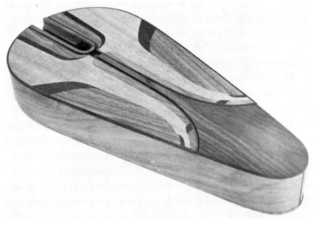

Above: By William Jaquith Evans. Distressed redwood case constructed and carved to hold the handmade raised sterling silver wine goblets. Felt lining is added where cups are placed. 11″ high, 20 1/2″ wide, 3 1/2″ deep.

Below left: By William Jaquith Evans. Ring display cabinet. Walnut. Dovetailed and assembled with four removable panels for displaying the rings horizontally. Each ring fits into a slot that has a hidden sliding bar that holds it in place.

Below right: Dulcimer case by Lawrence R. Jones. Brazilian rosewood, walnut, and mahogany. 6″ high, 13″ wide.

Above: Pipe holder (*two views*) by Skip Benson. American black walnut. 12'' high, 24'' wide, 14'' deep. Laminated endpieces assembled to flat sidepieces and shaped.

Courtesy, artist

Below: By William Jaquith Evans. Asparagus steamer (*closed and open views*). Laminated wood and metal. 12'' high, 18 1/2'' wide, 5'' deep. A funky object made as a joke; but it works.

MUSICAL INSTRUMENTS

The handmade musical instrument is a challenge for the craftsman to create. He must select woods that can be worked easily and will produce the necessary tonal qualities, that are lightweight, yet strong, and have a beauty of grain as well. It is likely that musical instruments actually existed before there were men to use them. Nature's own materials provide the ideas for many instruments. A split reed or piece of loose bark set vibrating or swaying by the wind produces sounds along the same principles as the reed or bark used in making present-day clarinets and oboes.

There are volumes written about the history of musical instruments and their creation. Modern craftsmen utilize elaborate examples and proceed to simplify them or add their own interpretations to the shapes, the ways they are finished, and to the cases that carry them. J. B. Blunk handcarves redwood root for percussion instruments; Trevor Robinson uses a lathe and some hand carving to create sleek, clean clarinets and flutes; Lawrence Jones, Peter McQueen, Harriet Matthews, and Capri Taurus's stringed instruments are one of a kind, lovingly made, constructed and carved pieces.

Above: West African thumb piano. Wood with metal. 2" high, 10" wide, 4" deep. Played to keep evil spirits away.

Collection, Mr. and Mrs. W. Chapman, Solana Beach, California

Whistle. Brazilian rosewood. Hand carved, with reeds pegged so they hang free within each end to produce sound.

Collection, author

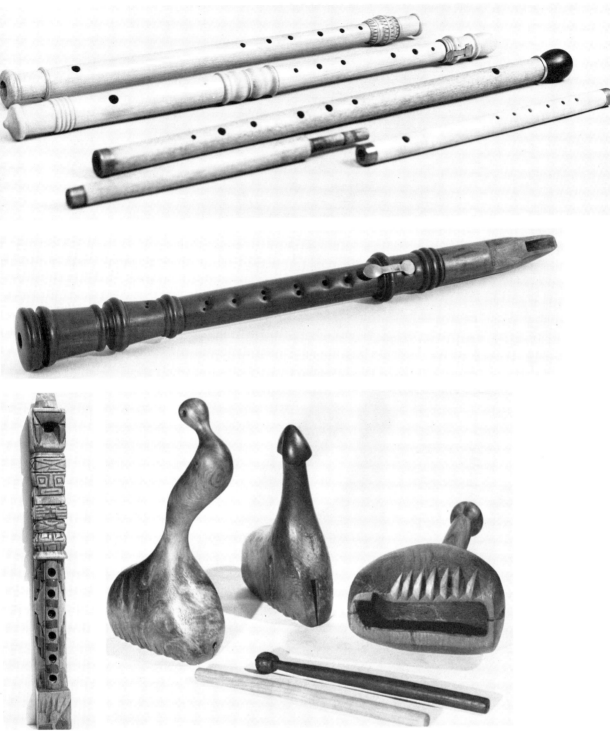

Above: By Trevor Robinson. Lathe-turned and hand-finished flutes (*top*) in various woods. Clarinet (*below*) of cherry wood. 17'' long.

Courtesy, artist

Left: Bolivian flute, carved and painted with added mouthpiece and reed. 12 1/2'' high, 1 1/4'' square.

Collection, author

Right: By J. B. Blunk. Redwood root. The instruments are played by hitting one side as a drum and by rubbing the stick along the toothed side for a grating sound. Heights: 10'', 11'' and 12''.

Top and center: Musical instruments by Peter McQueen. *Left to right, front and back views:* Mandolin, six string guitar, six string guitar, and twelve string guitar. Woods are teak with vermilion inlay, vermilion with maple inlay, walnut with multi-fancy inlay with either maple or mahogany necks. Sizes are from 10″ x 26″ to 13″ and 34″.

Courtesy, Deson-Zaks Gallery, Chicago, Illinois

Below left and right: By Lawrence R. Jones. Dulcimer with a soundboard of Sitka spruce, fingerboard of Brazilian rosewood with ivory inlay, and sides and back of Brazilian rosewood. Case is made of koa and Brazilian rosewood. 3″ high, 38″ long, 12″ deep.

Courtesy, artist

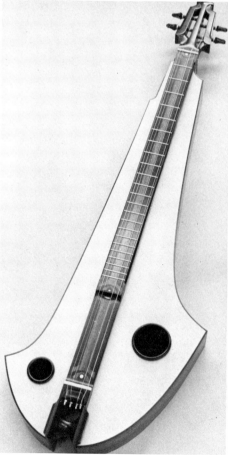

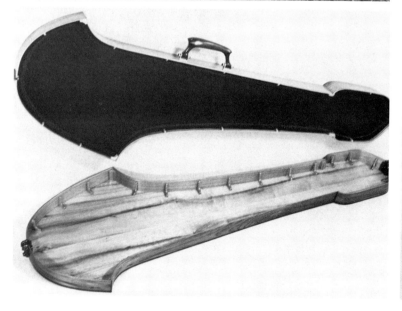

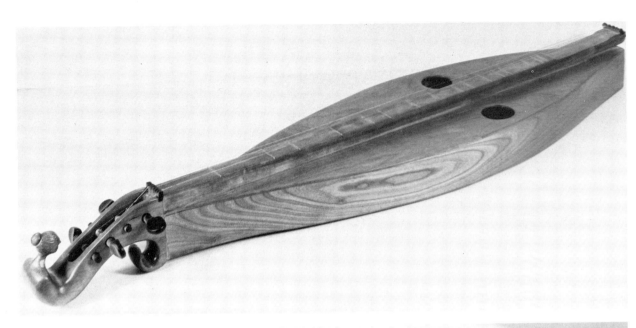

Dulcimer by Capri Taurus. Rosewood, ebony, and spruce.

Courtesy, Stephen Jackel,
Capri Taurus Dulcimers,
Felton, California

Top and below right: By Harriett Matthews. Dulcimer of cherry wood using a heat bending technique for the sides. 2 1/4'' high, 34'' long, 7 1/2'' deep. Ebony pegs. Hand-carved figure at end.

Courtesy, artist

TOYS

Handmade toys are surely art, and like any other art form they can be ordinary or beautiful, simple or ornate. Actually, the first toys of prehistory are regarded by the art historian as "sculpture" and not toys at all. In ancient Egypt a high priest would literally climb into a religious object that had moving arms, heads, and mouths, and "play" with the parts just as with a toy. Some authorities even considered dubbing these as early "kinetic" sculptures. Whatever the classification, the creation of toys is the creation of functional sculpture and the examples shown emphasize that premise.

A toy can be carved out of a block of wood and the result can be as simple and abstract, yet recognizable, a shape as those made by sculptor Hugh Townley. They can be as intricately designed with each piece beautifully carved and joined to others as those by Stephen R. Johnson.

Many craftsmen make toys simply because they are *fun*. Then they discover that handmade toys sell despite the colossal toy manufacturing industry. They discover that children gravitate toward the natural wood, hardcrafted object, while parents who buy toys believe the child prefers the gaudy, brightly colored plastic replica of a real object. One craftsman always lets the child for whom he's making a toy select the colors, and invariably they will be quiet, muted tones.

In designing toys, several factors come into play. The theme must be simple so the object is recognizable. It should capture the mood and concept of the real object without locking in the imagination too closely. When designing, you must decide on the proportions, amount of detail, weight, and texture.

It is best to design from the real object rather than from another toy. If you're going to design an airplane, look at real planes to determine the relationship of the wings to the body, the height of the piece, the shape of the front and the tail and roughly determine the basic proportions. If you plan to give it human characteristics such as eyes, month, and so forth, make these humorous and emphasize them.

Sketch the object and then edit out the details, keeping just enough to capture the concept and eliminating extraneous ones. Cut the pattern out of paper if you like and then trace, or sketch it onto the wood and cut out the parts needed. Tack the toy together and make sure it looks right, that all the parts fit. Assemble it, glue, sand, and finish.

There is little in toymaking to limit your imagination. If you are stifled for ideas, ask children what they would like for toys. Have them sketch their own idea. Wayne Kreuger's hedgehog house (page 235) is an example of a sketch made by a child. Mr. Kreuger developed the custom-made toy from the child's drawing and created a house he could never have envisioned himself.

Types of toys, such as puppets, banks, puzzles, push and pull toys, can be culled from the toy shelves but for actual design, the one-of-a-kind toymaker can outcreate the manufactured item for quality of workmanship and the ultimate in a sculptural and functional form of art.

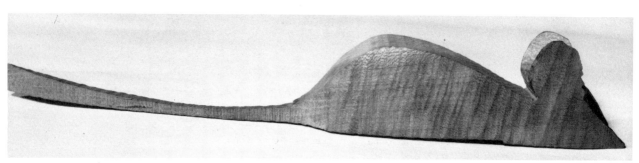

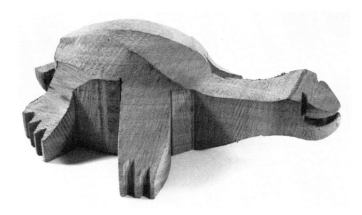

Opposite and top: Mouse and turtle by Hugh Townley exhibit minimal carving to capture the gesture of the figure. Mahogany.
Courtesy, artist

Other toys by Chuck Wiley are simply carved in stylized shapes with plywood wheels added. Light engraving, woodburning, and painting for details. Car of the future. Coupe and truck 9″ to 12″ long.
Photos, Fran H. Kumin

Top: By Jack Farris. Bird is made of seven different hardwoods. Willow body, African padouk comb, African satinwood beak, beech wings, rosewood pull knob, and walnut wheels. The snail shell is Hawaiian koa, head is African padouk, walnut wheels, birch and rosewood pull knob. Each is 7″ high and has eccentric rear end action.

Photos, Victor Joe Zell

Center: By Deborah D. Bump. A four-piece hippo puzzle assembled and apart. Animal-shaped laminated wood banks at right.

Courtesy, artist

Right: PORKY-PINE by Craig Carey. Hard maple with maple dowel rods. 5″ high, 7″ wide. The toy is also a bank.

Courtesy, artist

Above: ROCKA FELLA. Rocking peacock by Bob Daniells. Laminated and constructed red oak, Honduras mahogany, birch, and walnut, 48″ high, 38″ wide, 15″ deep. Tail (*detail photo above right*) made by insetting large and small circles.

Below: By Hanna Bauer. Painted puzzle. Shapes made on jigsaw and set in frame.

Right: HEDGEHOG HOUSE by Wayne O. Krueger. Assembled and carved painted wood designed from a child's drawing. 36″ high, 24″ wide, 18″ deep.

Photo, Jesse Alexander

Above: By Stephen R. Johnson. Dump truck. Yellow poplar. 6″ high, 16″ long.

Below: By Stephen R. Johnson. Train, yellow poplar. 4″ high, 17″ long.

Opposite top: THE CIRCUS by Daniel B. and Deborah D. Bump. Pine, mahogany, and bird's-eye maple.

Photo, Daniel B. Bump

Opposite center and bottom: By Stephen R. Johnson. Airplane of yellow poplar. 7″ high, 14″ wide. Crane truck of yellow poplar, 11″ high, 16″ long.

Left: Box. By Robert Herzog. Carved lift top lid. Koa. 8″ high, 8″ wide, 4″ deep.

Below left: Natural shape splash bowl. By Peter Petrochko. Spalted maple. 12″ high, 18″ diameter.

Courtesy, Snyderman Gallery, Philadelphia, Pennsylvania

Below: Venturi vessel. By Hap Sakwa. Maple, poplar, acrylic lacquer. 18″ high, 10″ diameter.

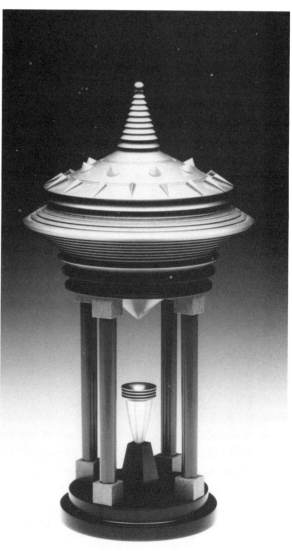

A Gallery of Containers & Other Objects

Russian caravan teapot. By Mike Darlow.
Painted wood. 14″ high, 14″ wide, 14″ deep.

Previous chapters have organized the objects by the techniques employed to create them: laminating, turning, carving, constructing, etc. Examples offered illustrate the techniques. In this gallery of examples, the method used is less important, though still evident in the organization. Constructed boxes are followed by bowls, followed by miscellaneous containers and vessels that illustrate new directions the forms are taking. Finally, a gallery of items is shown that defies categories. All illustrate the current state of the art; they offer inspiration for the woodworker and ideas for the collector to investigate.

Each artist, understandably and inevitably, has a feel for the material, a direction for the ideas presented, and for the forms chosen. These feelings are expressed beautifully through the medium and techniques. Often the artist can verbalize those emotions and attitudes, too.

Among woodworkers, there is an underlying reverence, a romantic, yet real respect for the material. There are those who explore the inherent qualities of wood to bring out its grains. Laboriously, but patiently, they sand and polish the surface to reveal its beauty. Others use the wood because of its infinite shaping potential and then paint the surface, ignoring the grains.

Michelle Holzapfel expresses feelings echoed in the works and attitudes of many artists who seek to explore the natural grains. She says, "The impetus behind my work is a desire to create forms that speak to the eye and hand, kindle the memory and spirit, and resonate in the heart as well as the mind. . . . As a material, wood is most satisfying, being simultaneously hard and plastic. It can hold an edge yet is not cold. Containing its own colors and patterns, it is true to the way it formed in growth. To let the material assert its woodness and still succeed in creating the desired form comprises the basic dialogue between material and maker."

Hap Sakwa, whose work has evolved into its current form through experience and change, now uses the wood to create the form, then paints the surface. He has moved away from the natural wood appearance for sculptural objects with which he built a solid reputation and an impressive body of work. He now explores the material in other ways (see pages 253–257).

Artistic inspiration takes many avenues. David Holzapfel says: "My work is inspired by the wondrous forms in which trees manifest themselves in Nature. Of no value to the lumber industry, unmanageable crotches, root systems, wolf or bull butt logs, dog legs, and burls are the gems with which I begin my work. Depending upon the message I get from the tree form, I will slice it into natural-edged boards, carve it, or cut it into blocks to be turned.

"Overall, the emphasis of my work rests with line and revelation of the integral beauty of 'tree,'" continues David. "The effort is one of collaboration. The natural expression of the raw material suggests the form within. I strive to develop that form. The material possesses an organic, wild-grained beauty. I seek to reveal this beauty and exalt it in the finished piece."

Love for woodworking that began with balsa wood buildings as a child fired Christopher Cantwell's woodworking career. It grew as he learned to use hardwoods and power tools as a teenager. He says, "In designing, I make it my ultimate goal to show the uniqueness of the fine woods I work. Since wood never has perfectly circular grain, I try to use flowing curves instead of circles. I maintain a natural harmony structurally as well as aesthetically by avoiding the use of metal fasteners or hinges. For each piece woods are individually chosen with consideration to color combination, figure, and grain direction."

For many artists, inspiration comes from exposure to cultural and traditional experiences with much emphasis on Japanese woodwork. William Jacquith Evans's current work explores the Brisé fan, long known in the Orient as a functional object on which lavish creative work is expended. Will's inlayed and constructed boxes (pages 98 and 105) evolved into new shapes and surface decor. Fans and their boxes are incredibly detailed (page 268). They are as unique to him as the Oriental fan is to its culture. In a similar evolution and unique result, David Carlin carves his interpretation of the Japanese netsuke (page 265).

The rich variety of work illustrated throughout the book—and in this gallery of examples for the new edition—reflect the visual creativity, fresh expression, and technical virtuosity found in the art form today.

Note: Photos in this chapter are courtesy of the artist unless otherwise credited.

Right: Lidded vessels. By Robert Herzog. Assorted hardwoods constructed, inlaid with carved tops. Sizes range from 11″ to 18″ high and from 4½″ to 7″ square.

Right below: A variety of boxes by Karen N. Hazama. Round box of padouk and ebony. 2″ high, 3½″ diameter. At right, a box to hold rattail files. Ebony. 1″ diameter, 4¾″ wide, ¾″ deep. Bottom is a rectangular box of ebony, 1¾″ high, 9⅝″ wide, 3¼″ deep.

Below: Jewelry chest. By Jere Osgood. Bird's-eye maple. Suede-lined drawers. Carved and constructed. 26″ high, 12″ wide, 12″ deep.

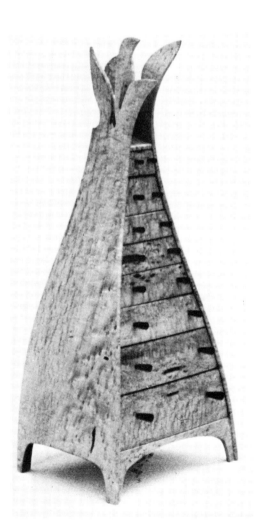

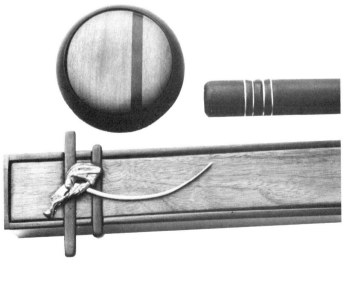

Chest #1. By Ian Forsberg. Amazon yellow-wood veneer, purpleheart tambour, and maple detail. 13″ high, 18″ wide, 20″ deep.
Courtesy, Snyderman Gallery,
Philadelphia, Pennsylvania

Silverware chest. By Charles Cobb. Narrow, northern California walnut, African wenge, about 900 birch dowels. 26″ high, 15″ wide, 13″ deep.

Photo, Mel Schockner

Chubb. By Robert Herzog. Constructed three-drawer jewelry chest with carved pulls. Joinery details add to the design. Koa. 8″ square.
Photo, artist

Earring box. By Charles B. Cobb. Hawaiian koa and African wenge. Nine pairs of earrings may be displayed through the glass top, which lifts off. Three drawers. Carving all around the box and the pulls. 15″ high, 15″ wide, 8″ deep.
Collection, M. E. Landes
Photo, Mel Schockner

By William Keyser. Rosewood and walnut box.
Approx. 2″ high, 12″ wide, 5″ deep.
Photo, Robert Kushner

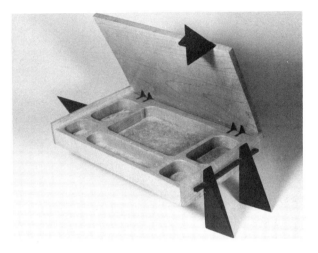

By Peter Vogel. Compartmented jewelry box
mounted on legs. Maple, purpleheart, and
ebony. 4¾″ high, 11¼″ wide, 6¼″ deep.

By William Keyser. Rosewood and walnut jewelry box. Approx. 1¾″ high, 6″ wide, 2″ deep.
Photo, Robert Kushner

Jewelry chest. By Christopher W. Cantwell.
Padouk, bocote, rosewood, ebony, and maple.
12″ high, 18″ wide, 9″ deep.
Photo, George Post

Earring cabinet. By Rosanne Somerson. Glazed and painted hardwood, padouk, handmade paper. 27″ high, 22″ wide, 7″ deep.

Detail (*below*) shows the divided drawers and painted half of a cup reflected in the mirror.
Collection, Ronald and Anne Abramson
Photos, Andrew Dean Powell

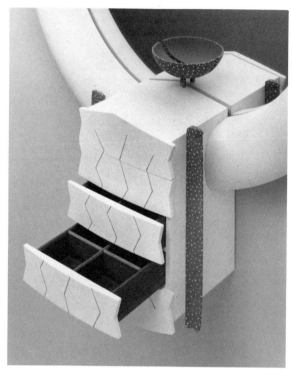

Jewelry box. By Ian Forsberg. Imbuya burl, blistered m'ninga veneer, paint, rosewood, mirror. 13″ high, 18″ diameter.
Courtesy, Snyderman Gallery,
Philadelphia, Pennsylvania

Jewelry box. By Ian Forsberg. Blistered m'ninga veneer, purpleheart tambour, and maple detail. 13″ high, 18″ wide, 20″ deep.
Courtesy, Snyderman Gallery,
Philadelphia, Pennsylvania

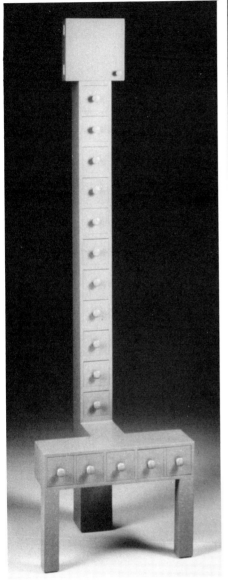

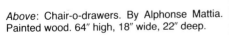

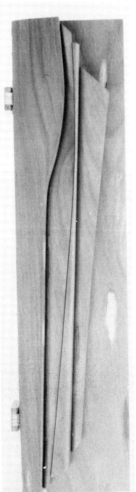

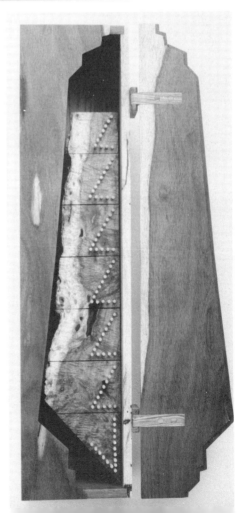

Above: Chair-o-drawers. By Alphonse Mattia. Painted wood. 64″ high, 18″ wide, 22″ deep.

Top right: Telephone cabinet. By Rosanne Somerson. Bubinga, painted wood, pink zebrawood. 31″ high, 24″ wide, 15″ deep.
Courtesy, Meredith Gallery,
Baltimore, Maryland
Photo, Andrew Dean Powell

Right: Wall hung cabinet; closed and open views. By Charles C. Cobb. African Padouk, Hawaiian Koa drawer fronts, tulipwood hinges, and ¼″ birch dowels as handles. 28″ high, 8″ wide, 8″ deep.

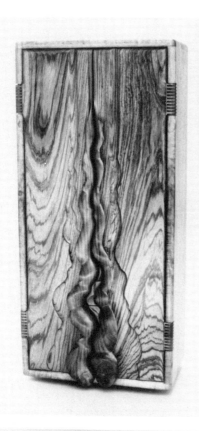

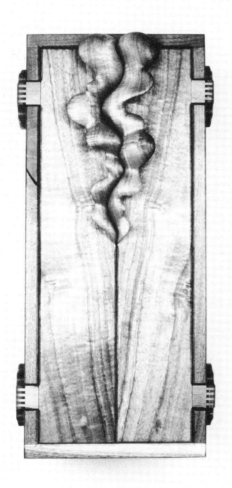

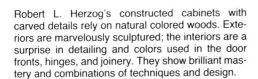

Robert L. Herzog's constructed cabinets with carved details rely on natural colored woods. Exteriors are marvelously sculptured; the interiors are a surprise in detailing and colors used in the door fronts, hinges, and joinery. They show brilliant mastery and combinations of techniques and design.

Opposite top: Wall hung cabinet; closed and open views. By Robert L. Herzog. Zebrawood, walnut, purpleheart. 30″ high, 14″ wide, 10″ deep.

Opposite below: Wall hung cabinet; closed and open views. By Robert L. Herzog. Australian blackwood, walnut, wenge. 24″ high, 14″ wide, 10″ deep.

Above: "Mini" wall hung cabinet; closed and open views. By Robert L. Herzog. 22″ high, 9½″ wide, 8″ deep.

Right: "Mini" wall hung drawers. By Robert L. Herzog. Walnut and koa. 22″ high, 9½″ wide, 8″ deep.

Photos, artist

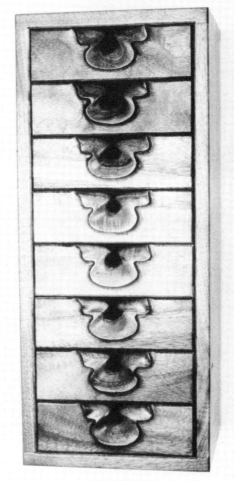

BOWLS

The bowls illustrated combine traditional face plate wood turning with other techniques, such as laminating, carving, and constructing. Ron Kent uses spindle turning methods for his large bowls, turning them until he achieves a paper-thin translucency. Virginia Dotson begins with a block of laminated natural woods and lathe turns a bowl but strives for form more than function. The colored laminates go all the way through the bowl and become three-dimensional. By working with this process and ideas for form, the finished bowls are more interesting than a more traditional laminated pattern on a flat surface.

Dennis Stewart's pieces are small and translucent, measuring no more than 6 inches high. The jewel boxes by Dale Chase emphasize a geometry in the surface treatment as a result of the special antique lathes used.

Top left: Translucent bowl by Ron Kent. Norfolk pine. The artist's challenge is a combination of beautiful shape and turning the wood until it is thin enough to be translucent when held up to the light. 8″ high, 18½″ diameter. At the maximum diameter, the wood is 0.10″ thick.

Collection, Edward Jacobson,
Phoenix, Arizona

Left: Ron Kent achieves shapes that are inordinately large as well as translucent. He is shown working on a 23″ diameter Norfolk pine log from a newly felled tree that weighs 120 pounds. The finished bowl was 18″ high, 20½″ diameter. it weighed 1 pound. Note that Kent uses spindle turning rather than a face plate. After turning, a "stem" is created with a hand grinding tool.

Above: Translucent bowl by Ron Kent. Norfolk Island pine. Lathe turned and hand rubbed. 10″ high, 3½″ diameter at bottom; 10½″ diameter at top, 0.07″ thick.

Collection and photo, artist,
Honolulu, Hawaii

Above: Large oval bowl. By Peter Petrochko. Padouk, purpleheart, rosewood. 10″ high, 14″ diameter.
*Courtesy, Snyderman Gallery,
Philadelphia, Pennsylvania*

Right: By Virginia Dotson. Walnut bowl with maple and wenge laminates. The color patterns go all the way through the bowl to become three-dimensional. 3⅝″ high, 10¼″ diameter.

Below: Fibonacci Bowl. By Michelle Holzapfel. After turning, carving is done with power and hand tools. Cherry burl. 4½″ high, 14″ diameter.

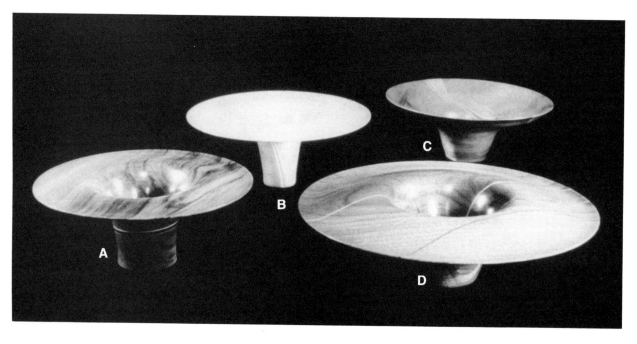

Four laminated bowls. By Virginia Dotson. **A:** African padouk with wenge and walnut. 3¾" high, 9" diameter. **B:** Cherry with maple. 3¼" high, 8¼" diameter. **C:** Honduras mahogany with cherry and maple. (See cover.) 3" high, 8¼" diameter. **D:** Red igem with maple and walnut. 2⅜" high, 10⅝" diameter.

Bowl. By Peter Vogel. Maple and purpleheart. 6½" high to top of points, 3½" high to rim. 9¾" diameter.

Cherry wood and glass bowl. By Ray Moszkowicz. Cherry wood with antique slumped glass inserts. 2½" high, 9¼" diameter.

Photo, artist

Translucent vessel collection. By Dennis Stewart. Lilac, Scotch broom, laurel. Turned vases displayed on an acrylic base. Sizes, *left to right*, 3″ high, 6″ high, 1½″ high.

Courtesy, The Hand and the Spirit
Gallery, Scottsdale, Arizona

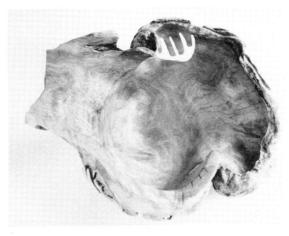

Hands bowl; inside view. David Holzapfel. Yellow birch. 16″ high, 26″ wide, 23″ deep.
Courtesy, Snyderman Gallery,
Philadelphia, Pennsylvania

Hands bowl, outside view (*see left*). Hand-carved details on the yellow birch wood.
Photos, D. Hard

Left top: Jewelry containers. By Dale Chase. Round boxes turned and ornamented with a Holzapfel lathe designed at the end of the 17th century and no longer made after the early 20th century. The various patterns or combinations of patterns are not possible with any machine made today. Blackwood, rosewood, and lignum vitae. The largest bowl is 3″ high, 3″ diameter.

Left center: By Karen N. Hazama. Walnut with ebony rim. 2″ high, 11″ diameter.

Left bottom: Pond Life. By Tom Rauschke and Kaaren Wiken. A container for wood and fabric inhabitants. Assorted woods, some glass and fabric. 6″ high.
Photo, William Lemke

Below: Sandhill Crane Egg. By Tom Rauschke. 11″ high, 5″ diameter. (See statement, page 262.)
Photo, William Lemke

Top: Perfect Reflection. By Hap Sakwa. The turned bowl shape was fragmented into slices and the parts reassembled in different relations from the original. Maple, poplar, polyester, acrylic lacquer, artist's manikin. 8½″ high, 18″ wide, 15″ deep.

Photo, Josef Kasparowitz

Bottom: Ventana. By Hap Sakwa. Poplar, acrylic lacquer, Liquitex. 4½″ high, 15″ wide, 15″ deep.

Photo, Josef Kasparowitz

MISCELLANEOUS CONTAINERS AND VESSELS

Containers and vessels whose shapes do not conform to a traditional box or bowl are often termed containers. Vessels are more akin to the vase shape. These may be functional or they may be called containers or vessels for lack of a better name. Such objects may be designed to be more sculptural than functional. They exist to express an idea, to become a beautiful work of art. Form is the important consideration. The interior "containing" space may hold an object created by the artist, as in some of the works by Tom Rauschke and Kaaren Wiken.

Woven vase. By Michelle Holzapfel. Burled red maple. 18″ high, 11″ diameter.

Collection, Nathan Ancell, Connecticut
Photo, D. Hard

Lightning vase. By Michelle Holzapfel. 14″ high, 10″ diameter.

Photo, D. Hard

Left: Siam. By Hap Sakwa. Maple, poplar, acrylic lacquer. 17″ high, 10″ diameter.

Photo, Josef Kasparowitz

Below: Container of 1,000 Future Dreams. By Hap Sakwa. Maple, poplar, steel, acrylic lacquer. 20″ high, 12″ wide, 9″ deep.

Photo, Josef Kasparowitz

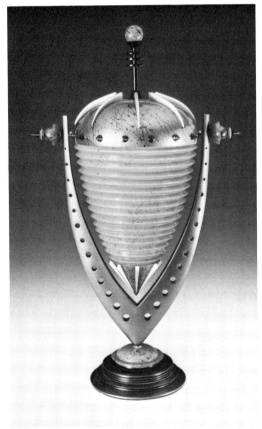

Statement from Hap Sakwa:

"I have chosen the more difficult route of personal expression through the total control of form, texture, and color. The freedom of not being limited by the demands of the material and its already sensuous textures and surface designs have added incredibly to my growth as an artist. My current use of wood is solely as a structural building material and that the sensual qualities inherent in the character of wood are no longer a factor in the designs or construction of my work."

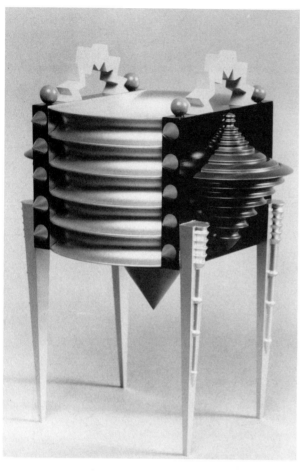

Newtron. By Hap Sakwa. Maple, poplar, acrylic
lacquer. 15″ high, 12″ wide, 9″ deep.
Photo, Josef Kasparowitz

Kandinsky. By Hap Sakwa. Maple, poplar,
acrylic lacquer. 10″ high, 9″ diameter.
Photo, Josef Kasparowitz

Vehicle vessel. By Hap Sakwa. Maple, poplar,
acrylic lacquer. 16″ high, 15″ diameter.
Photo, Josef Kasparowitz

Tar-an-tula. By Hap Sakwa. Maple, poplar,
acrylic lacquer. 12″ high, 13″ diameter.
Photo, Josef Kasparowitz

Top: Made in Oakland. (*Top view*) by Dennis Morinaka. Laminated bamboo, bamboo, Japanese silk Accede, hand marbled paper, lacquer. 5″ high, 28″ wide, 9″ deep.

Center: Made in Oakland. Right side, open view of above.

Photos, artist

Bottom: Noah's Runabout. By William Keyser. Assorted woods. 9″ high, 40″ wide, 20″ deep.

Photo, artist

Statement from Dennis Morinaka:

"I have been working with bamboo extensively and mixing media using a wide variety of materials. Most of my pieces now incorporate a cantilevered half section of bamboo as a kind of trough. I have designed a 'cover' that rolls back in the reverse manner of a rolltop desk (my inspiration). Current work utilizes thin laminated strips of bamboo which sort of houses the end of the laminated bamboo section. Each piece is highly polished and lacquered."

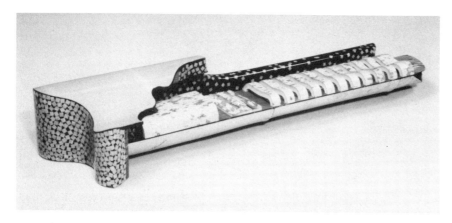

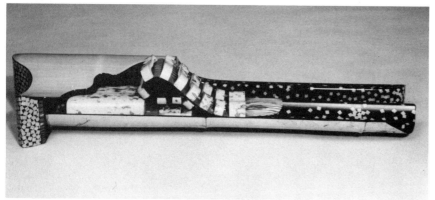

Top: Taking a Look At Self. By Michael N. Graham. Bleached basswood. 6″ high, 8″ deep, 10″ long.
Photos, Tim Hearsum

Center: Open view of above. Each side has a drawer.

Below: Circle/Square/Triangle. By Michael N. Graham. Bleached basswood. Container has a drawer that pulls out at each end. Closed view (*right*) and detail (*left*). 4½″ high, 10″ deep, 23″ long.
Photos, Tim Hearsum

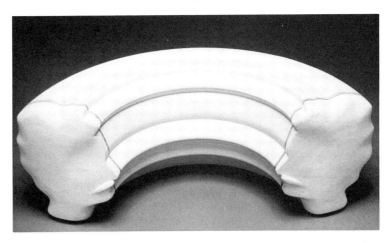

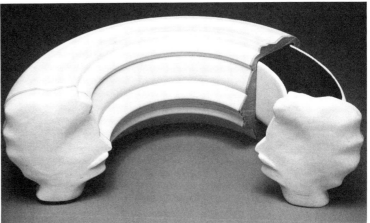

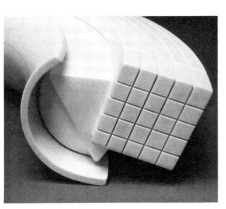

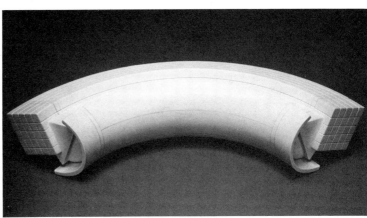

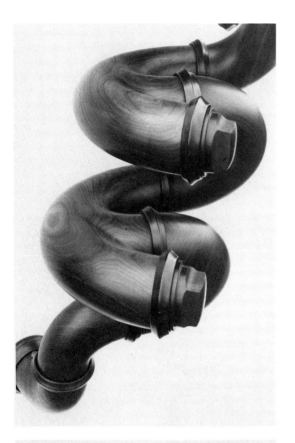

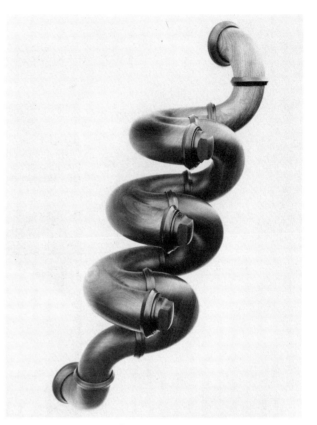

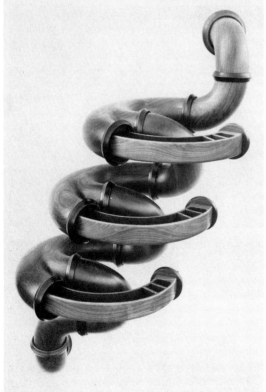

Spiral pipe form. By Michael N. Graham. Walnut and East Indian rosewood. Wall mounted container. 48″ high, 24″ wide, 24″ deep.
Collection, Irving Lipton, Encino, California
Photos, artist

Detail (*left top*). Open view (*left below*).

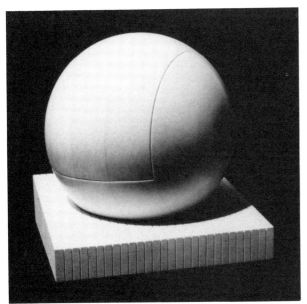

Statement from Michael N. Graham:

"These recent works have come out of my continuing interest in the container/sculptural form. About these pieces:
Circle/Square/Triangle [page 259, bottom] is an off-the-lathe geometry with a high ratio of function to mass. The Sphere/Square container is a stark gold color, a quiet geometry evolved to a color grid. And the spiral pipe, [opposite page] Why not?"

Sphere/Square. By Michael N. Graham. Three views. Closed, top lifted, drawers opened. Bleached basswood and acrylic lacquer. 10″ square.
Collection, Irving Lipton, Encino, California
Photos, artist

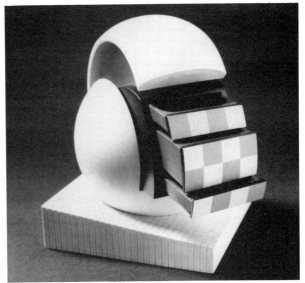

Lotus with Fish. By Tom Rauschke. Hardwoods. 14″ high.

Photo, William Lemke

The Universe. By Tom Rauschke and Kaaren Wiken. Varied hardwoods with feathers and objects. 18″ high.

Photo, William Lemke

Statement from Tom Rauschke:

"My recent work has focused on the lathe turning process, the act of bringing order out of chaos. I'm enjoying a simplified interest in circular shapes using the concept of a functional container as a departure point to explore further possibilities in wood. The full, round forms are an excellent vehicle to display the beautiful patterns and colors of wood grain. But each piece must also be worked beyond the basic object to become something very special and unique. The incorporation of my wife, Kaaren's, finely detailed embroideries in some pieces bring another element of color and design [see page 252].

"We bring to our work a sense of awe, humor, and vivid imagination. Experimentation and variation are also essential aspects that have resulted in numerous directions, offering a wide range of subject matter and personal interests. It is our life experiences that we symbolize in wood and fiber."

Ode to My Crystal Ladies. By Frank E. Cummings III.
Zebrawood, East Indian rosewood, ebony, ivory, glass,
24K and 14K gold, porcupine quills, quartz crystals. 32″
high, 7″ diameter.

Photo, Charles Blanton

Black Bottle, White Bottle. By Alphonse Mattia and
Jamie Bennett. Painted woods. Black bottle: 29″ high,
9″ wide, 4″ deep. White bottle: 26″ high, 7″ wide, 4″
deep.

Photo, Alphonse Mattia

Statement from Frank E. Cummings III:

"This piece is a visual ode that addresses a special
relationship between two people. The relationship is
symbolized, in part, by the purity and clarity of the
quartz crystals and the portraits on glass of a mother
and daughter. The form has an enclosure, secured by
a door, and a drawer: both with 14K gold capped
hinges and handles. The inner space is designed to
hold and protect mementos of the relationship. The
crowning effect at the top, symbolized by quills and
gold, represents the esteem in which the relationship is
held."

Top left: Tree jewelry box. By Jerry Patrasso. Bird's-eye maple for the "leaves," Bolivian rosewood for the tree "trunk and branches," and Brazilian canarywood for the "grass" base. 12¼″ high, 10″ wide, 7¼″ deep.

Above: Motor Head. By Stephen L. Casey. A "macho" jewelry box of walnut, padouk, purple heart, brass, and leather. The dashboard is a brass pinned, leather-lined drawer and below it is a carved change caddy. 15″ high, 13″ diameter.

Bottom left: Tribute to Friendship. Erika Wolfe. Jewelry box of rosewood and silver. The box parts separate and fold out to open (*below*). The base is woven silver wire. 6″ high, 3″ square.

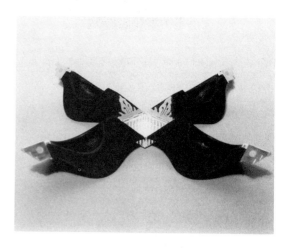

AND MORE

In this gallery you will find assorted functional objects that the artist has chosen to further an idea or simply to create, in wood, something not usually associated with the item. Bill Chappelow's apothecary scale (page 266), an object normally made of metal, becomes an étude, a composition in balances of ideas, form, and materials. Dale Binford's "Knightstick" (page 266) is a visual pun. Mirrors serve a practical use, but lend themselves well to wood frames and handles and backings. Toys and clocks in the hands of the fine woodworker become precious art objects.

Right: Barking Rocks, Seal Rock. By David Carlin. Mexican manzanita burl. 3⅛" high.
Collection, G. P. Frank
Photo, Sharon Deveaux

Far right: Barrel Full of Monkeys. By David Carlin. Manzanita burl. 1½" high.
Gerard Collection
Photo, Sharon Deveaux

Center right: 4th and Inches. By David Carlin. Boxwood. 1" high, 3½" long.
Gerard Collection
Photo, Sharon Deveaux

Below: The size of Carlin's objects can be better appreciated by seeing them in the artist's hands, in progress. He works on "A Rat on a Ghost" and studies the shape of a skull to incorporate into his miniature carvings.

Photos, Nickolas King

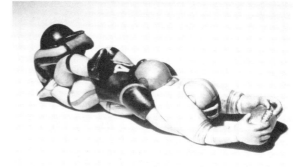

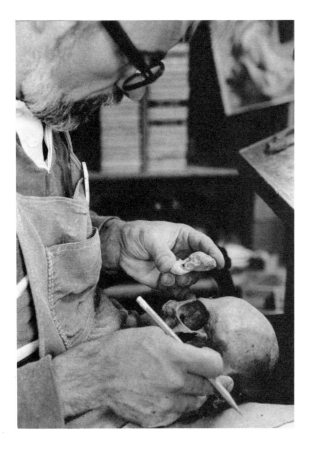

Above: Knightstick. By Dale Binford. Tulipwood, silver, copper, leather. 20″ long.

Left top: Sushi set for two with chopsticks and condiment dish. By Tony Lydgate. Rosewood and bird's-eye maple. 1½″ high, 13″ wide, 6″ deep.

Photo, George Post

Left bottom: Apothecary scale. By Bill Chappelow. East Indian rosewood. 8″ high, 6″ wide, 6″ deep.

Whale bell. By Dale Binford. Amaranth, silver, garnets. 5″ high.

Top right: Carved pull toy. By Jack Farris. Varied colorful woods. 12″ high, 10″ wide, 6″ deep.
Photo, Victor Joe Zell

Center right: Tractor. By Bill Chappelow. Live oak, white oak, red oak, pernambuco, beechnut. 8″ high, 11″ wide, 6″ deep.

Below right: Burl and spalted clock. By Peter Czuk. Maple. 3″ high, 5″ wide.
Courtesy, Mindscape Gallery, Evanston, Illinois

Below: Clocks. By Tom Thresher. Thin wooden discs rotate to tell the time instead of conventional clock hands. Various woods with wood inlays.
Courtesy, Mindscape Gallery, Evanston, Illinois
Photo, George Post

Top: Fans and fan boxes. By William Jaquith Evans. Fan of the Sarcophagus, at rear. Assorted woods are used for inlay and parts of the Brisé fans and for the matching fan box. Each box is shaped to fit the closed fan exactly; the cover replicates the fan blade design. A pull-up lining of hand-stitched suede cloth is on the bottom inside of the box; when lifted it reveals a pattern of the fan with each part labeled as to the type of wood. There is a "collector" listing within, also, as each fan and container is signed by the artist, numbered, and cataloged. Sizes vary from about 8″ to 15″ high.

Below left: Phases of the Moon. By William Jaquith Evans.

Below: Detail of the inlay work in Fan of the Sarcophagus (*above*).

Top right: Mirror. By David Van Nostrand (Interpreta Woodworking). Walnut. 18″ high, 30″ wide.
Courtesy, Snyderman Gallery, Philadelphia, Pennsylvania

Center right: Mirror. By David Van Nostrand (Interpreta Woodworking). Oak burl. 27″ high, 33″ wide, 7½″ deep.
Courtesy, Snyderman Gallery, Philadelphia, Pennsylvania

Below right: Hand mirrors. By David J. Marks. Brazilian rosewood with birch inlay, some ebony for detailing. 14″ long, 6″ diameter at mirror end.

Below: Talking House Candelabra. By Rosanne Somerson and Jacqueline Ott. Heads can be rotated to face away or toward each other. Long square open box in center provides candle storage. Painted and glazed wood, patinated copper. 46½″ high, 19″ wide, 11″ deep.
Collection, Bernice Wollman and Warren Rubin, Workbench Gallery, New York Photo, Andrew Dean Powell

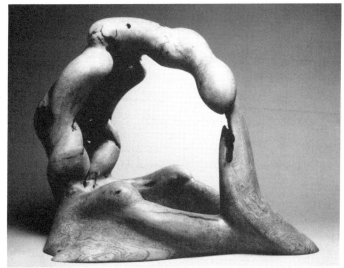

Selected
Bibliography

There are many more books available in each category listed below. Consult the library references: *Subject Guide to Books in Print* for current books, and *The Cumulative Book Index* for current books and books that are no longer in print but still available through libraries.

I. WOOD TECHNOLOGY

Beekman, W. B. *Elsevier's Wood Dictionary*, 3 volumes. Amsterdam, London, New York: Elsevier Publishing Company, 1964.

Berry, James Berthold. *Wood Identification.* New York: Dover Publications, 1966.

Constantine, Albert, Jr. *Know Your Woods.* New York: Charles Scribner's Sons, 1959.

Dechamps, Roger. *How to Understand the Structure of Hardwood.* Belgium: Musée Royal de L'Afrique Centrale. English translation, 1973.

Edlin, Herbert L. *What Wood Is That?* New York: The Viking Press, 1969.

Hackett, Donald F., and Spielman, Patrick E. *Modern Wood Technology.* Glencoe, Illinois: Bruce Publishing Company, 1968.

Harrar, E. S. *Hough's Encyclopaedia of American Woods*, 13 volumes. New York: Robert Speller and Sons, 1957.

Hunt, George M., and Garratt, George A. *Wood Preservation.* New York: McGraw-Hill Book Company, 3rd edition, 1967.

Sloane, Eric. *Reverence for Wood.* New York: Ballantine Books, 1965.

II. WOODWORKING

Brown, Emmett and Cyril. *Polychromatic Assembly for Wood Turning*, England: published by The Society of Ornamental Turners. n.d.

Campkin, Marie. *Introducing Marquetry.* New York: Drake Publishers, Inc. n.d.

270